THE REACH OF SOLITUDE:
The Paintings of Ann Taylor

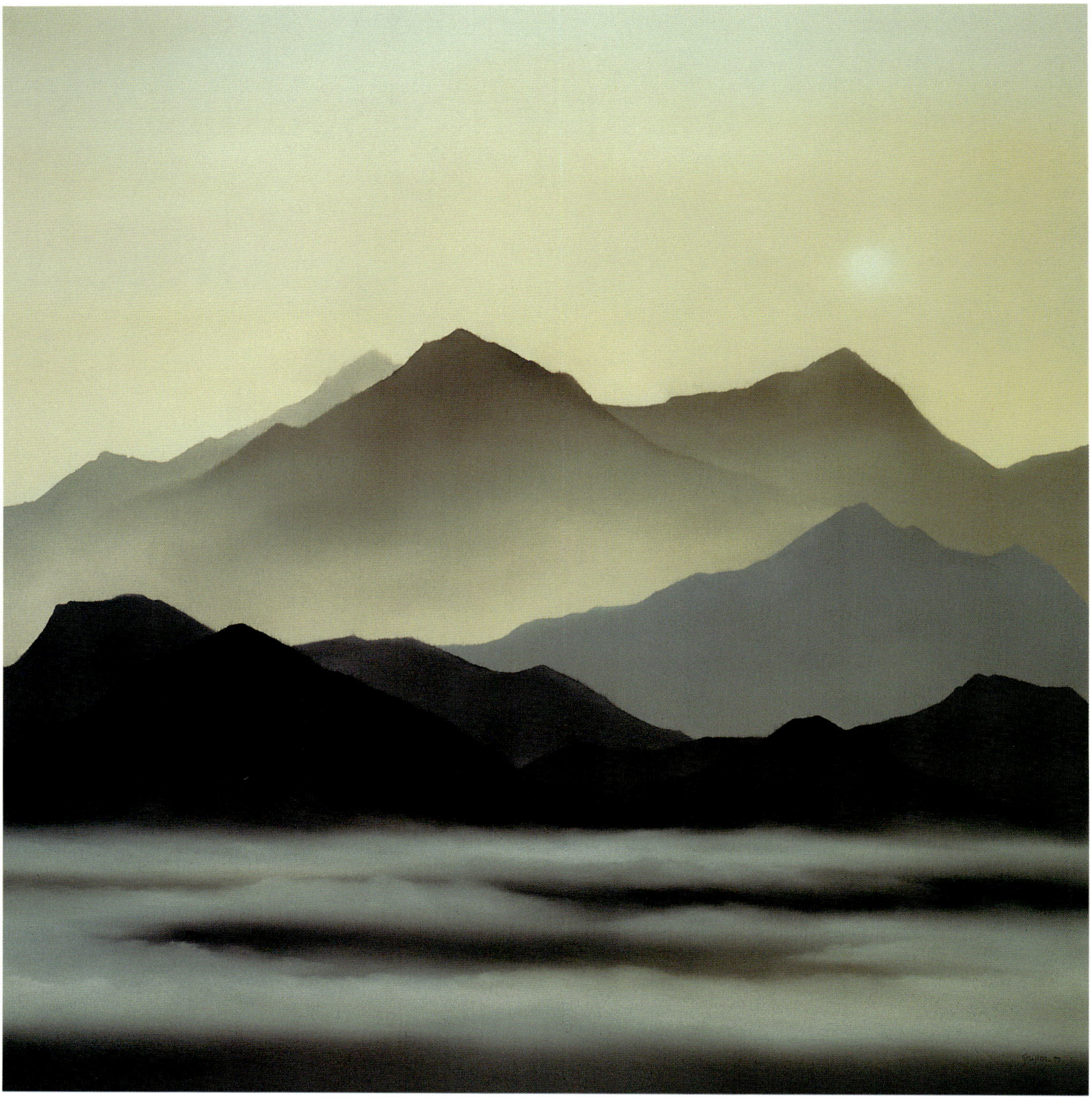

THE REACH OF SOLITUDE:
The Paintings of Ann Taylor

Text by Barbara Cortright

Paul S. Eriksson
Publisher
Middlebury, Vermont

Frontispiece:
Umber Peaks 1977
36″ by 36″
oil on canvas

Manufactured in the United States of America.

Library of Congress Cataloging in Publication Data
Cortright, Barbara.
THE REACH OF SOLITUDE: The Paintings of Ann Taylor

1. Taylor, Ann. 2. Landscape painters—United States—Biography. I. Title.
ND237.T374C67 1983 759.13 [B] 83-1700 ISBN 0-8397-7073-1

Contents

Foreword

Several things remain in my memory from the early seventies when I met Ann Taylor and first decided to represent her work. The paintings were objects of delight clearly conveying her spiritual attachment to the landscape. I was also impressed by her professionalism and the care with which she executed the paintings. Furthermore, they were as serene and beautiful as the artist herself.

Landscape is the source of her work. She concentrates on a portrayal of the natural world through the use of light, color and line. But her work is also magical and mystical. Through her imagination she re-creates those things which have a life and structure different from our own.

Her awareness of underlying natural forces and rhythms allows the viewer to experience the earth's beauty without the gravity of man's presence. We glimpse at the power of nature, alive and harmonious in spite of its own turbulence and ceaseless change. Immediately identifiable objects and natural forms are rendered in a lucid abstractness. In a Taylor work the ephemeral and the perpetual forces combine in a seemingly effortless way.

For the past decade I have watched her paintings evolve as she herself has grown. The same dynamic compositions and subtlety of tones are as important to her now as they were when I first met her. This book testifies to the continuing vitality of Ann Taylor's art.

George Henoch Shechtman
Director, Gallery Henoch
New York

Introduction

One of the main features of the contemporary art of the Southwest is the profound stylistic change which has taken place in the work of so many of the artists who live here. Some of them vividly recall the precise moment the transformation occurred, while others have clear accounts of the event or series of events which triggered it. They describe the sensations of "before" and "after" and note that the change in artistic style was an integral part of a bigger shift in personal outlook which had culminated in an unexpected but exceptional identification with the sociology and geography of the Southwest.

This phenomenon has been observed to occur with such frequency that there is the strongest temptation to develop it into a theory to be applied to all artists who live here. These artists, however, are far too individualistic for such easy theorizing. Whatever might be the pictorial motives they use, whatever might be the compelling influences which the region has exerted on their work, many of them should really not be regarded as southwestern, regional artists. The new awareness has merely liberated their instincts thereby producing a body of work having greater depth of meaning than that which had gone before.

In this regard, the paintings of Ann Taylor are particularly interesting and elusive. She has been living and working in Arizona for the last four years. By a simple demographic classification therefore, that should make her a southwestern artist. Added to this, the subjects she paints seem to be quintessentially characteristic of the geography of the area. Her canvases are filled with panoramic vistas: distant saw-tooth mountains silhouetted against huge skies, and between you the viewer and the endless horizons are shimmering mists and great oceans of empty space. There is the firm impression that here is yet another descendant of the Hudson River School but in decorative modern dress.

Up to quite recently it would have been relatively easy to identify a Taylor painting. All her landscapes looked as if they had been poured through a sieve of rose-colored glasses. The American wilderness was tamed to such a degree as to become perfectly civil, even though remote and detached. Yet in real life these gentle, pastel-colored western hills have taken many lives. In the Southwest the word for this hostile terrain is "awesome." Therefore, to see her as simply a painter of the southwestern regional landscape, when none of these qualities appear in her work, is to fail to grasp the true concerns of the artist.

Something in the translation of the natural forms hinted that there might be things going on in the works other than a romantic representation of mountains, skies and clouds. Perhaps it was the air of detachment; the pictures seem to insist on maintaining a fixed distance between the artist's conception and the viewer's needs.

Early in 1980, Ann Taylor began what she called the **Acceleration Series** of paintings. With these she gave notice that after twenty years she was ready to probe into an area with which her colleagues and collectors would hardly have associated her. These pictures were still landscapes painted with her flat, dead-pan brush. Reading from top to bottom, there was sky, then the typical saw-tooth mountains, and in the foreground, a road, the sides of which converged sharply as it moved swiftly away to the horizon.

These paintings contain two interesting features. One is the dislocation of the linear perspective so that the plane of the road is not parallel to the ground as it should be but parallel to the plane of the distant, curving sky. We see it twisting madly and falling out of the picture. The other and more remarkable feature is the presence of what one can only call a pregnant, empty space in the middle of the road. It is as though an object had been there but had moved off at a tremendous pace, accelerating as it gathered speed to vanish in the distance. Hence the title of the series.

In the best of these paintings, **Current Madness** and **Rotation,** the artist has succeeded in articulating the "form" of the empty space. This might seem to be a rather pedantic contradition, but it is perhaps the only suggestion to be put forward to explain the liveliness of this ostensibly flat area. In discussing this point with me, a close friend of the artist remarked, in a brilliant flash of insight, that the empty areas were like "the noise you hear just after the music has stopped playing."

Despite these innovations, however, the **Acceleration** paintings still belonged to the earlier work. They still had that easy, drawing room comfortableness about them. But, the compositional possibilities they opened up led on to the next piece which was crucial to the work as a whole.

When Ann Taylor came back from her European trip in 1981, she made a small lithograph of Stonehenge, the famous pre-Celtic archeological remains in England. It showed two images of the huge monoliths standing stark against an extremely simplified, totally abstract background. The tendency towards abstraction had always been an integral part of her domestic environment and in her thinking about art but had never found expression on her canvases. The Stonehenge print proved a perfect excuse to take a decisive step in this direction.

A number of transition pieces followed where she literally divided the canvas into two rigidly geometric areas similar to the format of the print. These areas were separated by an edge as straight as a die and as hard as steel. This was the catalyst the system needed. By some mysterious chemistry I do not fully understand, the hard edge, introduced not for its own sake but as a necessary concomitant of the compositional structure, released her passion for pure plastic relationships in the business of picture making. It set off a bomb under the works and the Taylor oeuvre was changed, utterly.

In the early paintings, the lack of "texture and quality" was always baffling. After Tachism, Matter painting, and the various modes of Abstract Expressionism, every artist under the sun is aware of "paint quality" insofar as it reveals the inner workings of the artist's emotional responses. But to all enquiries on this matter Ann Taylor gave the firm answer that she was "not interested in that kind of autobiography."

The latest of these paintings, **Window with Pink Shimmer,** is an austere composite of the two elements, the one naturalistic, the other abstract, which were first identified but not isolated in the **Acceleration Series.** This picture is a key work which completely vindicates the artist's position.

For instance, all the earlier paintings were done premier coup and the flat paint, flatly applied, remained flat. In the recent paintings, one effect of having to deal with the new composition is that the artist finds she works over each separate area several times in order to bring them into harmony with each other. The infinitely graded sfumato tonal areas, built up in carefully applied discrete layers of paint, now have a quality of paint which is extremely beautiful. But this quality, as the artist has been saying all along, has nothing to do with "autobiography."

Secondly, because each area is masked out and repainted several times there is a microscopic shift in the position of each edge every time this is done. Therefore, instead of being a mere edge, that is, the boundary between two fields of color, it is now a visible line varying in mass and linear quality. It is a line of great beauty. But it does not leave the canvas and come out to the viewer. It is reticent to the point of being completely self-effacing. We now know the reason for the non-naturalistic color, for the sense of remoteness and detachment. We are being presented not with natural phenomena, but with a state of mind. This is the oriental philosopher in a western guise.

The present path of development upon which **Window with Pink Shimmer** is just at the halfway mark has all the possibilities of evolving into a major body of work. Alas, in this department, it is not possible to predict. History is full of artists who, at a given point in their careers, have moved up, backwards, sideways; some have with a crunching suddenness ceased working altogether. If **Window with Pink Shimmer** could not have been predicted, either by her colleagues, her collectors or her galleries, the artist does not appear to have had any such doubt or uncertainty at all. In her own mind, to use a phrase common in British Imperial politics, it was the inevitability of gradualness which has led to what I have been calling the breakthrough.

This small but timely monograph celebrates the crossing of an important watershed in the career of Ann Taylor. The next year or two will see where this direction will have led.

Donald Locke
Phoenix, Arizona

Illustrations

THE REACH OF SOLITUDE:
The Paintings of Ann Taylor

Chapter One: The Paintings' Nucleus

". . . it meant getting up really early, mostly in the dark, and watching the dawn. Everything changes from black to silhouette to color. I loved it. I didn't care if I saw the birds so much as if I saw the light."

As a young girl, Ann Taylor longed to go along with her father on birding trips. It was not the birds but the wide, expanding world out there she wanted to see. In her imagination, these trips would take her into light and space and freedom, the experience all the more soaring and magnificent for being in her mind. When she became an adult and was at last allowed to go along, reality did not let her down. She found that having waited so long made her interest all the keener: "The places, the country itself, were very beautiful. We went to a particular ridge in the Appalachians where the hawks all funneled through. The light over that Pennsylvania farm country changed nearly every hour." For Ann the birds were pretext. It was not seeing hawks that excited her, but the wonderful vistas in which she saw them—the light-filled skies which, in time, would appear in her paintings.

In fact no birds at all came to fly in her paintings, nor did any particulars of time or place pin the landscape to identifiable locations. Now, looking back, she sees birding as simply an experience of nature, an experience that dramatized light as it permeated atmosphere. It was this that became the dominant theme in the abstracted, universal landscapes which make up the body of her work.

Born in Rochester, New York, in 1941, Ann lived there until she was seventeen years old: "My first memories are dim and scattered . . . the converted farmhouse where I lived until I was six, mashed potatoes with crumbled bacon, a moosehead in the kitchen, the blue-figured wallpaper by my bed, a bull grazing in the ring next door and especially the long, cool light of winter and the dancing clouds of high summer."

Later the family moved along the road to a rambling, colonial-style country house. A long lane led up to it on a hilltop, surrounded by trees and gardens. Childhood years there were filled with an abundance of activities for Ann, her two brothers and her sister. That heightened hilltop view gave her a sense of separation from the others around and below her. In this sense of separation is to be found the standpoint of Ann Taylor, the artist—felt if not analyzed—the psychic ground from which many of her paintings would be conceived. It was appropriate, even to be expected, that in roaming in this idyllic countryside Ann should lie down in a field or a meadow and encounter the words of a great American individualist: "I was thirteen at the time. The field seems, in memory, to be filled with hundreds of butterflies and tiny flowers. The air was steamy and languorous with the smell of newly cut grass. One side of the hill looked out at the Conners' woods, a place of mystery, dark with giant trees and the dankness of the creek. It was on that hillside that I first read Ralph Waldo Emerson. It was as though I was reading my very own thoughts, an affirmation of self-reliance and the power of the individual."

Although Ann's life was not without people, not isolated, it was in these moments of treasured solitude that her clearest, most vital impressions were formed—impressions always associated with the natural world around her but centering finally on her inward receptivity.

For Ann, then, that country, Rochester and its surroundings, not only supplied the setting for her childhood but also furnished the background from which her first work would be shaped: "The early paintings, if they are derivative from anything, are derivative from this experience of nature. Above all they came from the land I knew best, the area around Rochester, the southern shore of Lake Ontario and the Finger Lakes. There, because the water creates a pervasive cloud cover, the predominant color is gray—gray in all its shades and gradations."

These memories fed the fund of images, the capital from which she had to draw. In her mind's eye, light became color expressed in the subtlest of modulations: "Light has always been of extreme importance to me. And color. But light and color are only singular elements in the myriad of components which compose a painting. For me, a good work of art must contain the intellectual, formal considerations of line, form and design. Light and color produce an emotional response, design a more analytical one. If a painting doesn't have this complexity of parts, I think it fails to be a significant work of art."

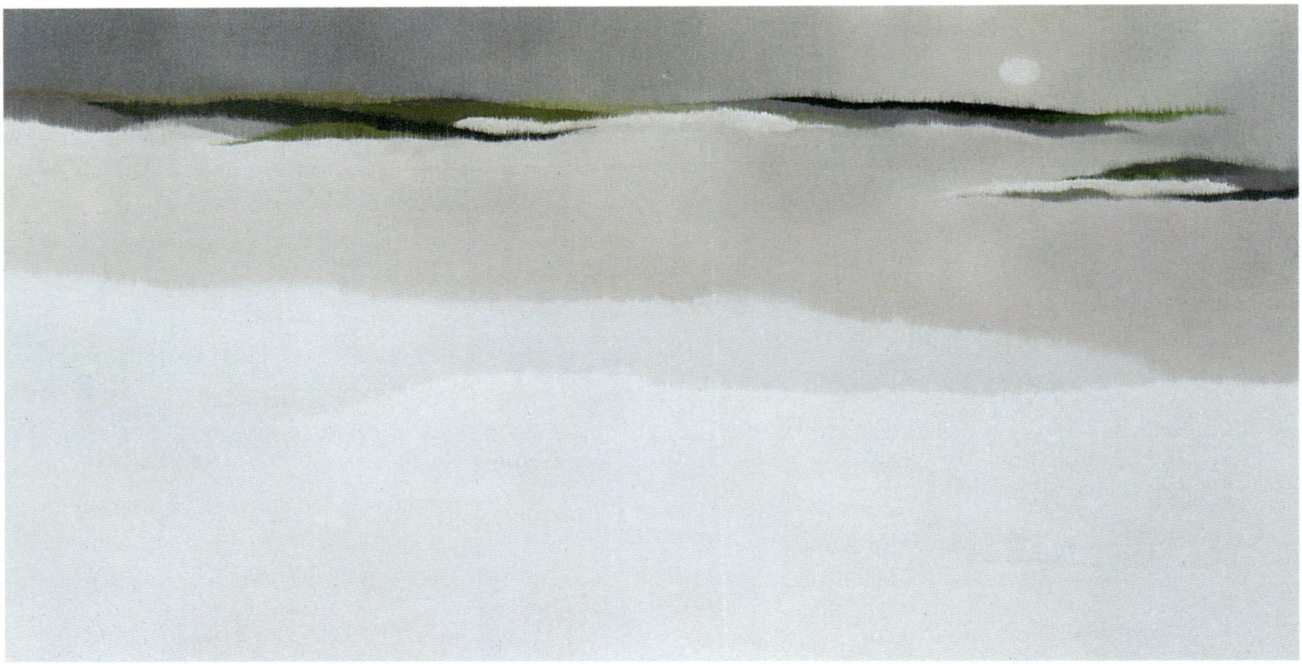

Early Thaw 1967
24″ by 48″
oil on canvas

Early Thaw presents the young artist's awareness of such an intention. Here the scalloped bands of earth are high in the background, allowing the minimal foreground and middle ground to dominate the picture. It combines a series of whites grading through the most delicate changes to become white on white. The natural prototypes are obscure, simplified nearly to the point of non-referential abstraction. Had the painting not been given a landscape title, the implication of melting snow and bands of green would have been much less clear. Yet the feel of winter, with the white disc of the sun and the fringed contours which appear as vegetation, gives **Early Thaw** the attributes of northern lands, growth sprouting in a chilly sun. It is a painting honed to elementals. A few evocative strokes suggest a plain; the wide field of foreground snow is scarcely indicated by the form, but the suggestion opens up the eye to a sweep of space—the void which is packed with meaning. Given these references to the natural world, it can nonetheless be appreciated for its careful design—a horizontal layering detailed by the overlapping of large and small triangular shapes.

Upstate Winter 1972
36″ by 40″
oil on canvas

A collage of fine variations was extracted from Ann Taylor's childhood experiences and continues to be threaded into her paintings. **Upstate Winter,** for instance, draws vividly on those remembered Rochester winters. The painting makes a first impression of vast fields of snow. The atmospheric effects of those overcast days are described in the subtle movement of one gray into another. The horizon is high on the picture plane, and the landscape itself spreads across the middle ground: rolling fields, hedges and patches of shadow cast on the hills. Additionally, it exists as a strong compositional study. The use of a series of triangles, built up one against the other, leads the viewer from right foreground to left background and back across the horizontal sky. It is also a private image—the isolated, unpeopled landscape is a perception of the artist.

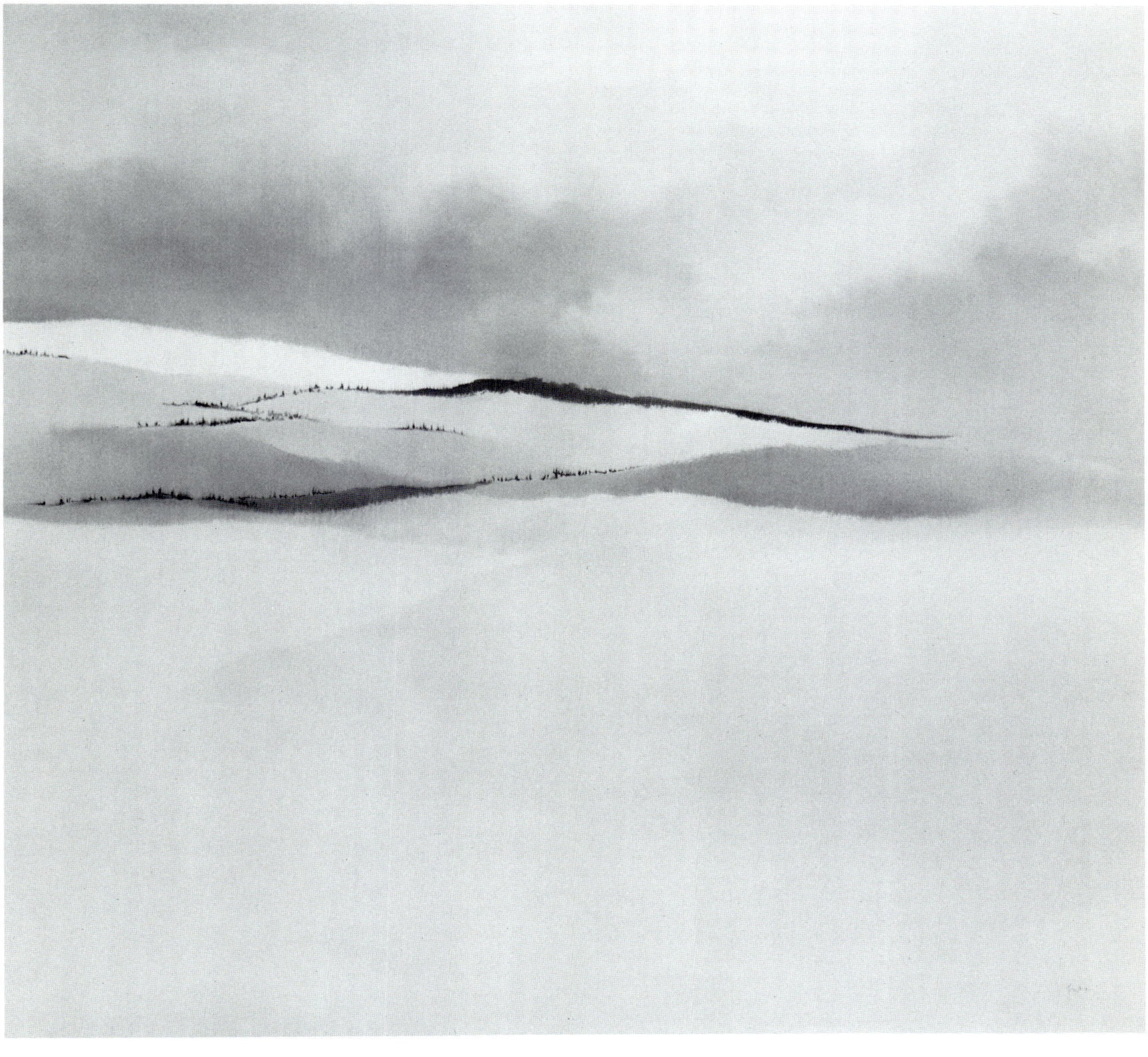

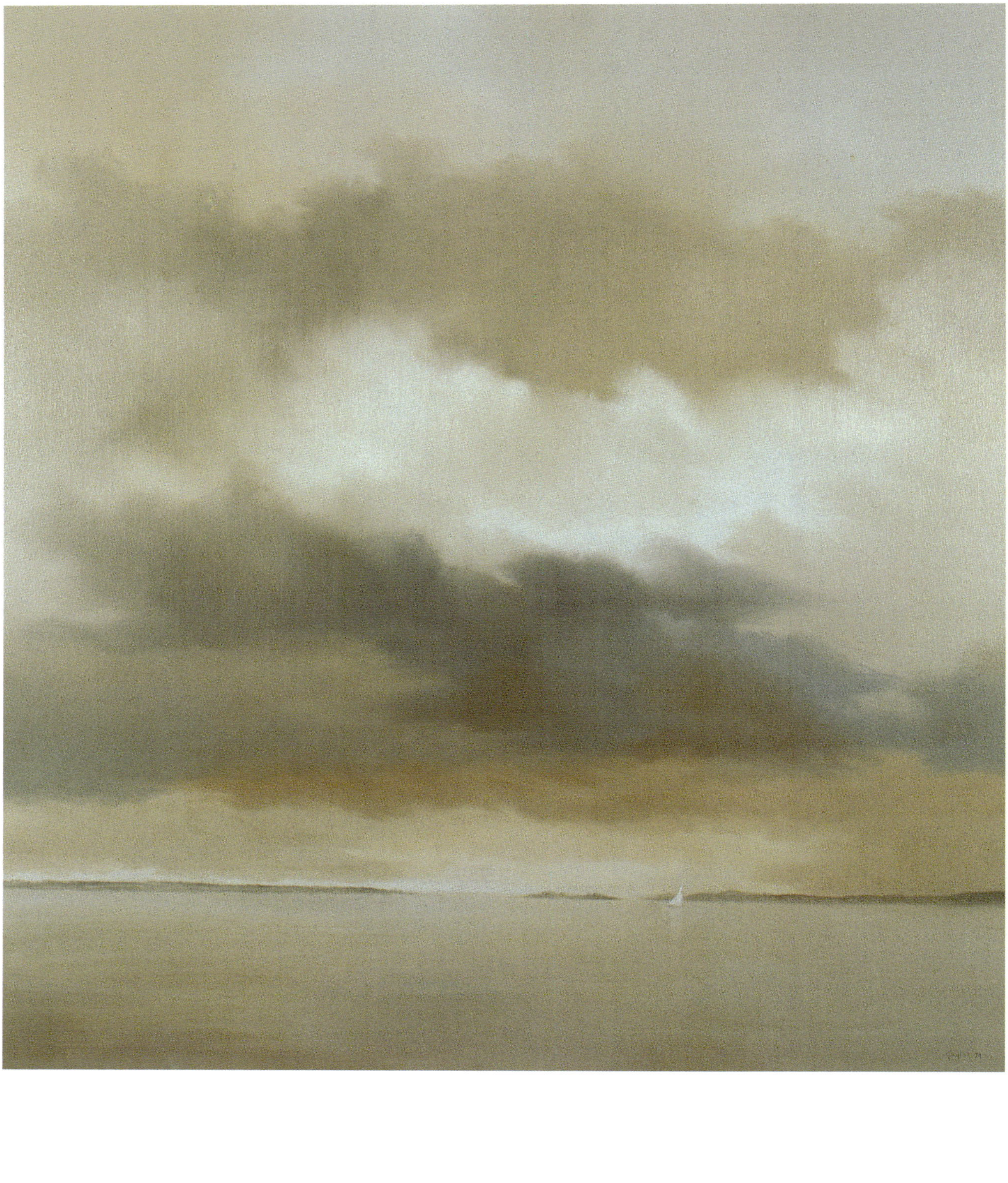

In her stored memories, besides the impressions of land and sky, there is water—a recollection of summers in the forties and fifties spent on Higgins Lake in Michigan. The house was a family place, the sort where summer gatherings of relatives were held, but the memory Ann keeps most firmly in her mind is of time spent alone by herself: "We had a pavilion with a dock that stretched out into the lake. I remember sitting for hours on the end of it watching the sky and listening to the water. In the pavilion I lay back on one of those old-fashioned swings made of logs, to do my dreadful summer reading. The water and the sky distracted me. As I remember it, the sky was always intensely blue, filled with huge stacks of cumulus clouds. Although actually I have never painted the lake representationally, some of my work has been touched by its beauty."

Clearly, the sensation of sky and water, resolved through the lens of memory, was a continuing theme in Ann's paintings. **Michigan Sail One** is such a painting. It is one of several paintings executed in memory of her uncle: "He sailed on that lake. I never attempted to recreate anyone else's feelings about that place but, in this case, I knew that he felt as I did. As it happened I did the painting in colors that do not relate to Michigan at all, yellow and brown and gray, but it was appropriate that in this painting they were that way."

Michigan Sail One 1974
38" by 36"
oil on canvas

Characteristically, this was a matter of color determined by mood, not natural circumstance—a consistent principle in Ann Taylor's paintings. Events transmuted through emotion determined this arbitrary palette. This practice, traceable in the early paintings, is a key to succeeding ones: not nature's colors, but colors relating to its imprint on the artist's mind were the ones she selected.

Again, a sense of solitude informs the painting. A single boat, very small, is alone on a vast expanse of water, a mirroring vault for sail and sky. This unpeopled quality, remarked by most observers, is distinct from the idea of loneliness: "I think of Munch and Hopper when mention is made of loneliness. I certainly don't think of myself in those terms." Rather a theme of self-reliance, of drawing on Emerson, is her pervading attitude.

But **Michigan Sail One** was painted years after the birding expeditions and years after Ann's summers in the log swing beside the lake.

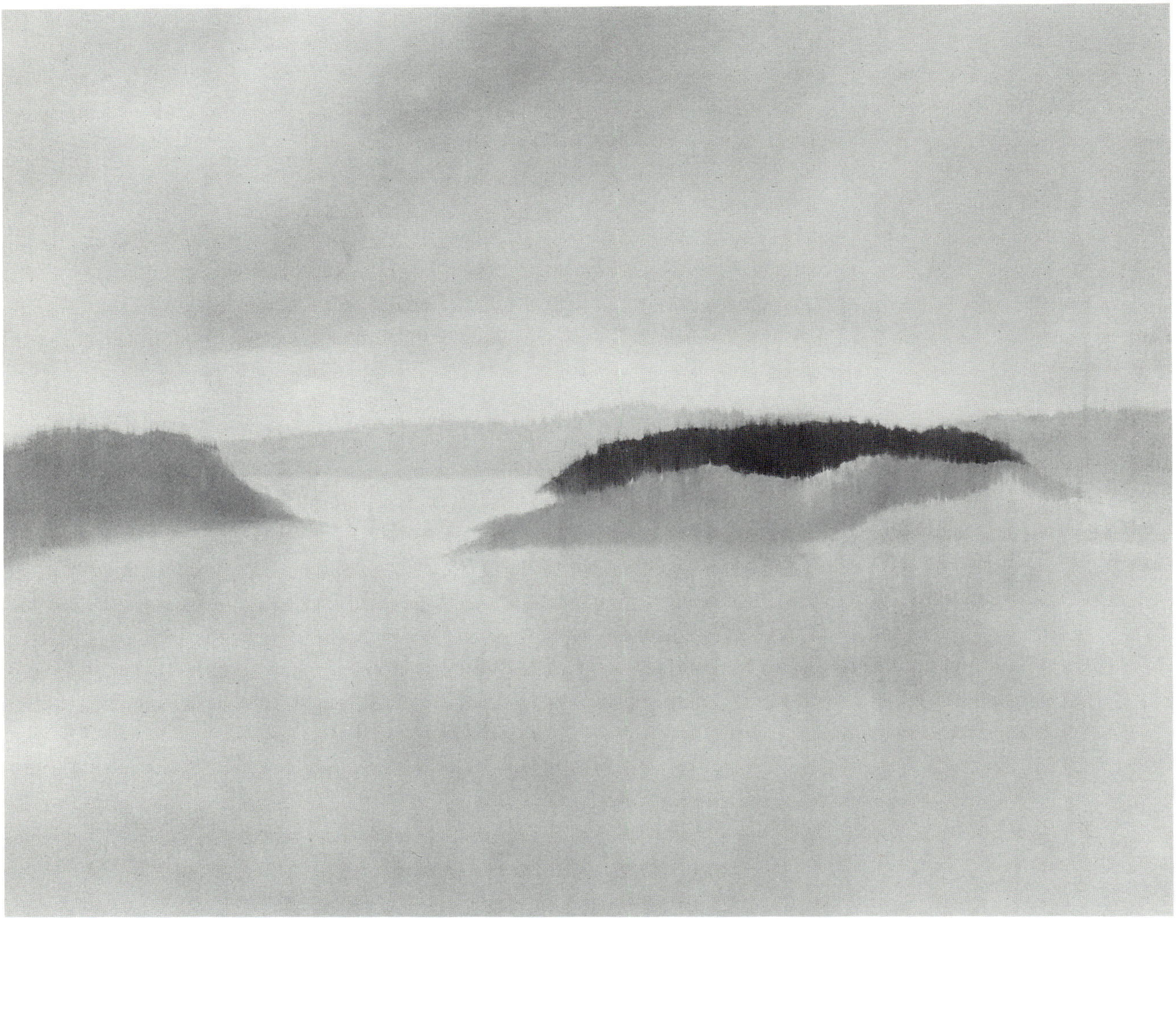

Lake Dawn 1965
28″ by 36″
oil on canvas

An antetype, a much earlier painting, is **Lake Dawn,** also conceived from recollections of a lake, though this one is Lake Placid where she spent many weeks in the summers of the sixties and seventies: "I went out fishing in the early mornings before breakfast. The glass surface of the lake reflected the soft Adirondack Mountains. It would break only momentarily when a cast lure indented it, then would instantly resume its sheetlike quiet. I painted that quiet, even when life was raging and shouting around me. It didn't really matter whether or not anything was caught (although more often than not someone brought in fish for breakfast). What mattered was being on the lake—a peaceful and immensely beautiful experience. I did little drawings with a ballpoint pen on my grandmother's stationery, outlines of the configurations of mountains as their reflections spread on the water."

Less subtle than **Michigan Sail One, Lake Dawn** is a matter of simply balanced space and form, a rather formal composition. Even so, and in spite of the fact that the Taylor finesse at painting clouds which are almost palpably atmospheric had not appeared yet, the foundation of this formal arrangement is the evident insistence on extracting pattern from natural phenomena. This is a working base for all her paintings, including the later ones of clouds. Essentially the pattern here is determined by stripping down the forms to the simplest possible: a thematic shape is selected and repeated, here a sort of truncated cone, visible right side up in the water and reversed in the sky above it, combined with a long, undulating form, like waves or shoreline.

Testifying to the continued influence of nature, however filtered by the artist's individual perception, **Placid Three** records again the impression of being out on the lake in the slow diffusion of the early light.

Of course fishing, like birding, was a pretext. It was secondary to Ann's aesthetic goals. Nevertheless, her appreciation of the splendor of natural phenomena was heightened by these moments in the wilderness. On Lake Placid, the mist was of special fascination: "It rises in beautiful plumes and just evaporates before your eyes. I will never forget the mist at dawn slowly dissipating, making the water a mirror for shapes and colors. **Placid Three** is an exploration of reflected light and reflecting water. It is also a painting which treats atmosphere as a veil. I want the viewer to penetrate the veil before understanding on a more cerebral level how the work is put together."

Placid Three 1965
26" by 28"
oil on canvas

Again, the sun is felt as white light, as penetrating radiation. The palette remains restricted, somber bronze and gray. The view is an interior perception rather than a reiteration of the natural world.

Another element apparent in this painting, which was to remain consistent in Ann's later work, is reductiveness. To remove detail, to order her work, her days and the way she lived them in balanced segments were a part of life as well as art for the artist. Her paintings and the style in which she lived reflected her desire to rid herself of extras, to remove the foliage, as it were, and see the branches.

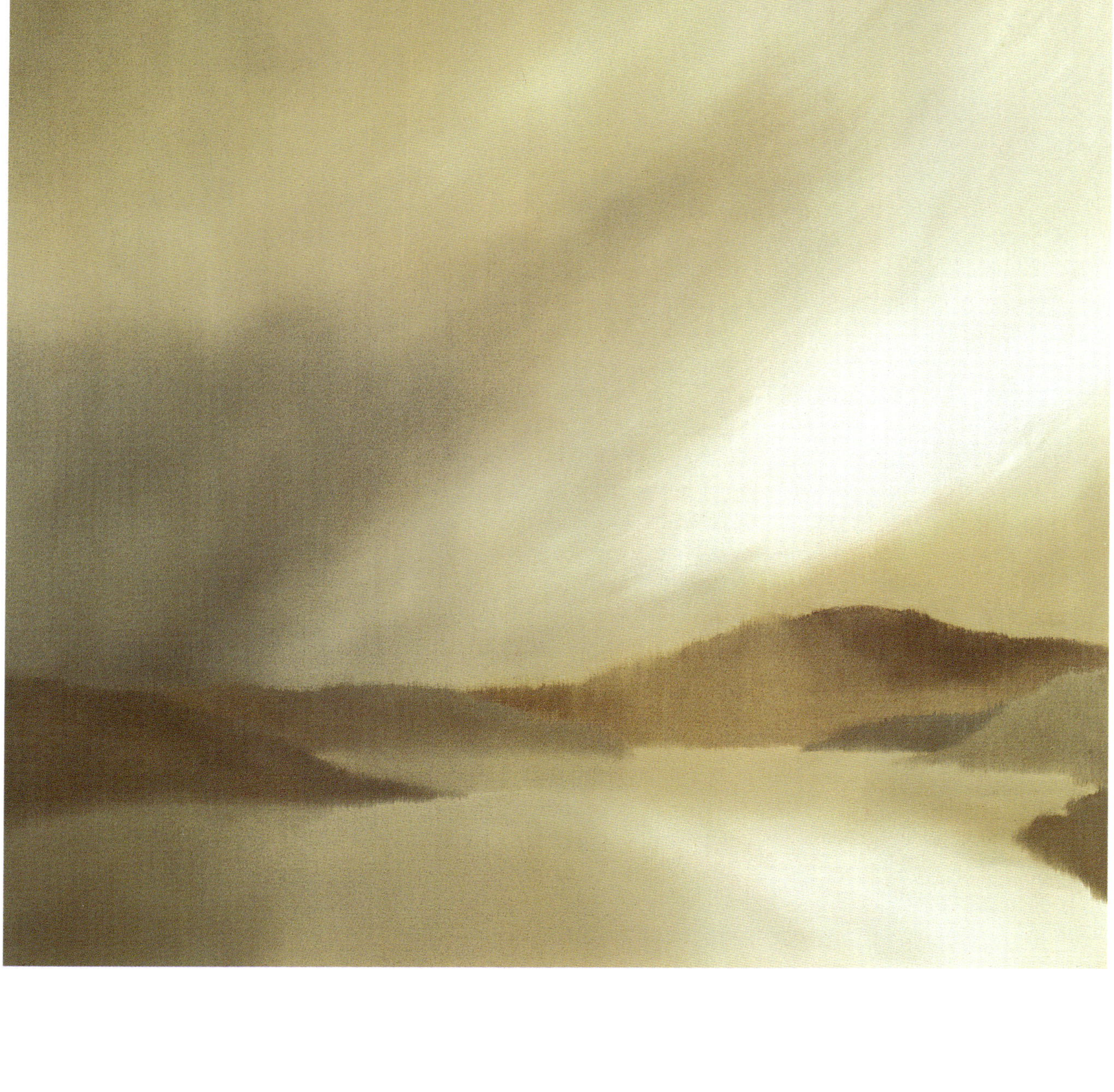

For example, in 1958 when she left home to go to Vassar College, she remembers: "I went with the definite feeling that I wanted to live in a very sparse environment—monkish. I removed the institutional furniture from the room and adopted a kind of living space that was oriental in its simplicity."

Alongside this urge for simplicity was the still deeper impulse to work alone, to explore independently. Ann's will to paint, in fact, had been stimulated by a particular event, an explosion of silent feeling set off by the happenstance of an unexpected gift: "My mother had majored in art history and was talented herself. My parents did not collect art then, although they had nearly papered the house with my father's collection of Audubon engravings. One Christmas, when I was eighteen, I was given a set of oil paints. I don't think my mother had any particular thought that I would be so taken by it. I went back to college that year with the box and the canvas boards and just fell in love with it. I was totally absorbed. It was like opening a door."

Ann had not gone to Vassar as a painter. At the time, she was studying voice and had been doing so for a long time, first at the Eastman School of Music in Rochester and then again at Vassar: "Singing and the study of music were my real loves. In college I was also writing poetry; in fact I was majoring in English and music. I published a few poems in the college magazine and started a small poetry anthology. This combination of interests is not rare. Singing, writing and painting are related; they are all methods of communication. In music, however, I was not a composer, I was a performer. Performance alone was not creative enough, but the creativity involved in painting consumed me. I never had the belief in my writing that I had almost immediately in my painting. I never thought it was as original. I stopped my musical activities and my writing for many years and just painted."

But at Vassar the box of oil paints, small though it was, did not fit in. There was no room in her curriculum for classes in art. Ann painted alone in her room and tried to find her own way: "It was all very solitary. There were no mentors, no people to ask." Ann strove for simplicity in the work, simplicity in the life around her. At Vassar, where she did her painting in the same room where she slept, the connection was intimate.

Her intention broadened into clear vocation. But the road was far from marked. Lacking technical direction, her first efforts involved all manner of alternatives: "I found that there is a certain flexibility in the paint itself—certain accidents happen. At first I experimented. What happens if you brush or scumble? What if you paint on the back side of the canvas instead of the front? How does stain painting work? I tried every conceivable method. Sometimes if I got an effect that seemed to resemble a landscape I would amplify it. When I started purposely painting landscapes, I didn't want to paint anything else. The forms of the land are so infinitely various! The light in the landscape, in the sky and land and water, is all-pervasive. Landscape is non-narrative, non-programmatic. It doesn't have to be a specific place to make the viewer feel that he knows it. He knows it from his own interior; he doesn't need my direction, only my guidance."

The actual tools Ann used were varied, along with her methods. They included brushes of all sizes, from those with a few thin hairs to house-painting size, and sponges to apply wash in very thin layers. There was also canvas, primed and unprimed, or masonite, or glass on which to paint. In the physical process of working, accidents happened with the paint itself which were then absorbed as compositional elements. The observed scene was thus transformed both by intention and by the incorporation of these accidents.

Afternoon Pond is an example of this painterly exploration of accident, the way the paint behaved as it was brushed onto the canvas. It brings to mind James McNeil Whistler's statement on the "use of incident." Whistler made use of the principle of chance, of painting accident, in his famous painting **Nocturne in Black and Gold: The Falling Rocket,** 1868. Here, as in Taylor's **Afternoon Pond,** light as it penetrates the evening air is the main protagonist in the drama.

Furthermore, although he believed that accidental occurrences in paint should be augmented and explored, a painting by Whistler's definition was first an arrangement of form, line and color, not a reference to a subject. For both artists this was intrinsic in the expression of the idea as a whole. With experience, Ann found that her capacity to seize on formal suggestions implicit in tone gradations grew and developed.

Also evident in **Afternoon Pond** is the internal interpretation of subject matter, introducing the sense of ambiguity. The line between sky and water, cloud and reflection, foreground and background, is deliberately ambiguous. An atmospheric weight dominates the picture and is enhanced by a nearly monochromatic color scheme, thus the painting is transformed from narrative into internal vision: "Ambiguity is very necessary in what I do. It is a way to let the viewer in, to allow him to uncover the forms and their meanings in stages."

Afternoon Pond 1968
38″ by 32″
oil on canvas

Although the general framework of Ann's paintings, their mood tranquil and contained, took shape and solidified at Vassar, the image of the artist herself was not so readily harmonized with the pattern of life there. It seemed that her painting, with all its necessary paraphernalia, did not find easy room for itself in college housing. It did not conform. The person of the artist, too, was non-conformist: "The preppy little girl in the Shetland sweater and McMullen blouse I was not. My feeling of separateness on the campus was reflected in the way I chose to live and what I chose to wear. I often dressed in black, in capes. Today it might be different, but in the fifties it mattered that I didn't conform—that I drew into myself."

Ann felt it was time to look out and away, to find new viewpoints. A sense of freedom, always a strong need at this stage of life, seemed more necessary than ever to her in the light of campus life with its many hidden but inflexible restrictions.

She and Libbie Gerry, a gifted pianist whom she had met at Vassar, drove to the West Coast in the summer of 1960. Ann wanted to find out what the alternative culture there was all about. The trip provided another view as well—the bonus of new visions of the American landscape: "On the road for nine weeks, we clocked nearly nine thousand miles. I was introduced to the unparalleled variety of the American landscape. The Nebraska plains were as impressive as the Utah canyons. The sight of the land was so satisfying! I felt I could explore it indefinitely."

In the end, Ann found that the alternative landscape more than the alternative lifestyle left its mark. She retained a strong curiosity, a feeling of attraction for those farther ranges. They had taken firm hold of her imagination.

Later, in fact, she went on to experience even higher, more rugged mountains. In 1967 she traveled to Alaska for the first time: "Alaska leaves an indelible impression on everyone. It's so vast! The landscape is beyond monumental. Its changes are so various that they are hard to grasp. The preparation for this trip was extremely detailed for we planned to camp on the open tundra for five weeks. Near Mt. McKinley, beneath the striated whites and lovely grays of the Denali Range, we saw caribou, moose and bears. We were even lucky enough to see a wolf, although he was a bit close for comfort, actually standing by the tent. There are patterns and colors in the snow paintings of the late sixties and early seventies that were influenced by this extraordinary trip."

St. Elias Mountains 1967
24″ by 48″
oil on canvas

The contour of the towering Alaskan ranges appears in **St. Elias Mountains.** Here the nearly vertical thrust of the mountainsides themselves, and the patches of wind-swept rock which show through, contrast with the pale foreground. The overwhelming impression is of light bouncing off light from snow. The foreground is made vague through light dispersion and lies awash in shine: "In the Arctic it's almost as if there is no horizon. The sky is a white gray and the ground is a light gray. They almost merge together."

Alaska's distinctive landscape influenced her work. It is definitely seen in a much later painting, **B. C. Range.** The edges of the peak are sharply saw-toothed, the cloud layers are dense, as if bearing further loads of snow. What seems more fused, more characteristic of the mature Ann Taylor paintings, is the nearly illusionistic polarity between the moist, atmospheric clouds and the obviously sharp, hard surfaces of rock. Here is a painting that could lead the viewer to believe in the feel of cold air in his throat and on his frost-burned cheeks because it nearly breathes cold air and the blinking brilliance glancing off of snow.

B. C. Range 1978
42″ by 52″
oil on canvas

Travel, an experience in itself, led to new, freer painting, and to new decisions. After the summer of her first trip to the West in 1960, returning to the confining Vassar campus seemed to Ann even less acceptable than before. Among incidents that added to her negative feelings was a citation from the student government because of the "inflammability" of the turpentine in her room. The determined individualist successfully defended herself against this charge but, afterwards, feeling the accumulated burden of a clash of her own will with those around her, she decided that for her immediate future the die was cast. The college's refusal to widen her curriculum to include courses in art tipped the balance: "The feeling there was all wrong. I wanted to paint and study art and I couldn't do that at Vassar. I did not want to stay."

Following exams, she decided to leave. New York, she knew, was the place artists should go. New York was the place she went.

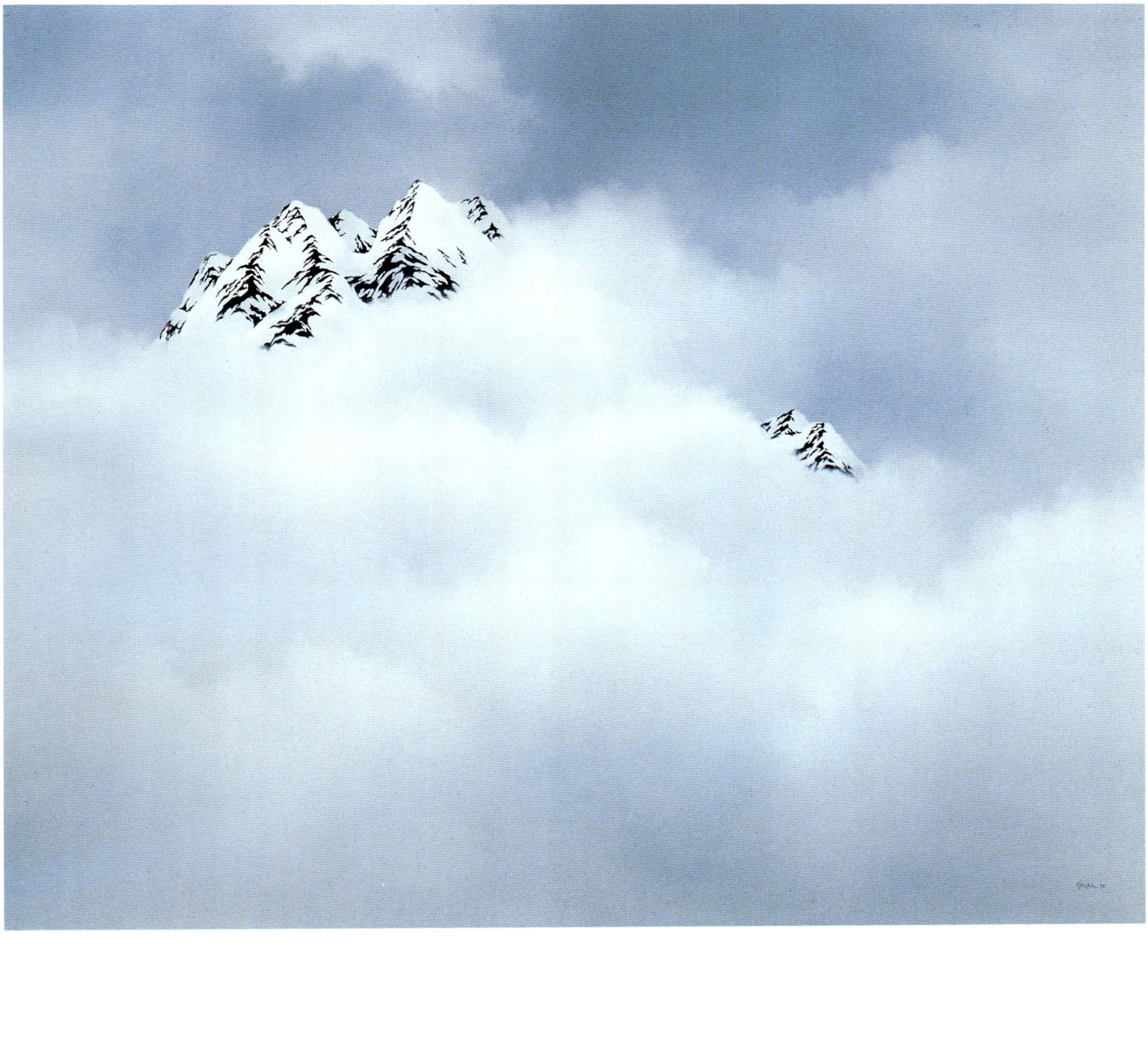

Chapter Two: New York, the City Phase

"Although I lived in the city, I never painted it, nor did I want to paint it. I was thoroughly enmeshed in the city's life and yet only its energy penetrated my art."

After Vassar, whose wide, tree-shaded lawns belied unseen but real enclosures, Ann emerged into the concrete confines of New York where, paradoxically, she felt free. Immeasurably stimulating, the crowded city with its quick pulse quickened her own: "I was attracted by the pace, the vitality, the availability of everything in superlatives—both the best and the worst. There is a fiery intensity about that city. The energy is compelling."

All the more compelling, though, was the need for respite, for the recreation of the stripped, ascetic space Ann had had in her simple dormitory room, her private eyrie: "My paintings are reflections of the solitary experience of life. In actuality, I have not lived alone since I was twenty. I was married for a long time, with additional people coming and going where I lived, but the insular quality of my life has nothing to do with that circumstance. It has to do with an inward feeling."

Ann's first step was to rent an apartment in Greenwich Village. She kept her few furnishings simple and low to the floor. Her aim was a feeling of openness. Later she would use this sense of uncrowded space in her paintings—the kind of space that, as in a Chinese scroll, assumes infinity but is narrow enough to be contained within its silk boundaries.

Restraints were dispensed with in her course of study too; the rigid curriculum was over. Ann enrolled in a figure painting class at the New School for Social Research, the school from which she graduated in 1962. The instructor was a painter named Julian Levi: "I don't know how old he was at the time—late sixties, probably—a wonderful man with the twinkling eyes of a Franz Hals portrait."

The class itself, however, posed problems. After a few sessions, during which Ann was dismayed when the instructor's assistant approached her canvas and painted on it himself, it was evident to her that every student in the room watched every other student, "all of them trying to paint like each other." This was not why Ann had come to New York, not the situation she had hoped to find: "I always thought that whatever I decided to do, it had to be unique. In painting, striving for my own style, my own identity, came before any other consideration." Clearly, something had to be changed.

Characteristically, Ann took the direct route and asked Julian Levi if she might bring canvases to him privately for a showing and critique. He agreed.

The paintings she had to bring, which she had done in her apartment, came together as a sort of overview of her experiments from the preceding year. Although the methods varied widely, they had a common attribute: in spite of their strong tendency to abstraction, they all bore a recognizable resemblance to landscape.

That landscape was invariably empty. No people inhabited it, nor was there any record of their passing through. There were no landmarks, no specified place or time. Rather there was the suggestion of clouds and atmosphere and long views to a horizon which could be anywhere.

One of these paintings, **Island,** a very early example, contains the seeds of this approach. It can be read as a spread of gray washes punctuated at the center by bright flamelike shapes, or it can be interpreted as sunset-reddened cliffs rising out of a steel gray sea. In physical terms, the sky is achieved through gradations occurring in the thinned pigment as it spreads on the canvas and the artist's decision to bring out these shapes. Most important to the total concept is the lightest gray above the sea which becomes cloud shot through with light. Light as the focal point of a painting became a constant in her later work.

Island 1961
30" by 24"
oil on canvas

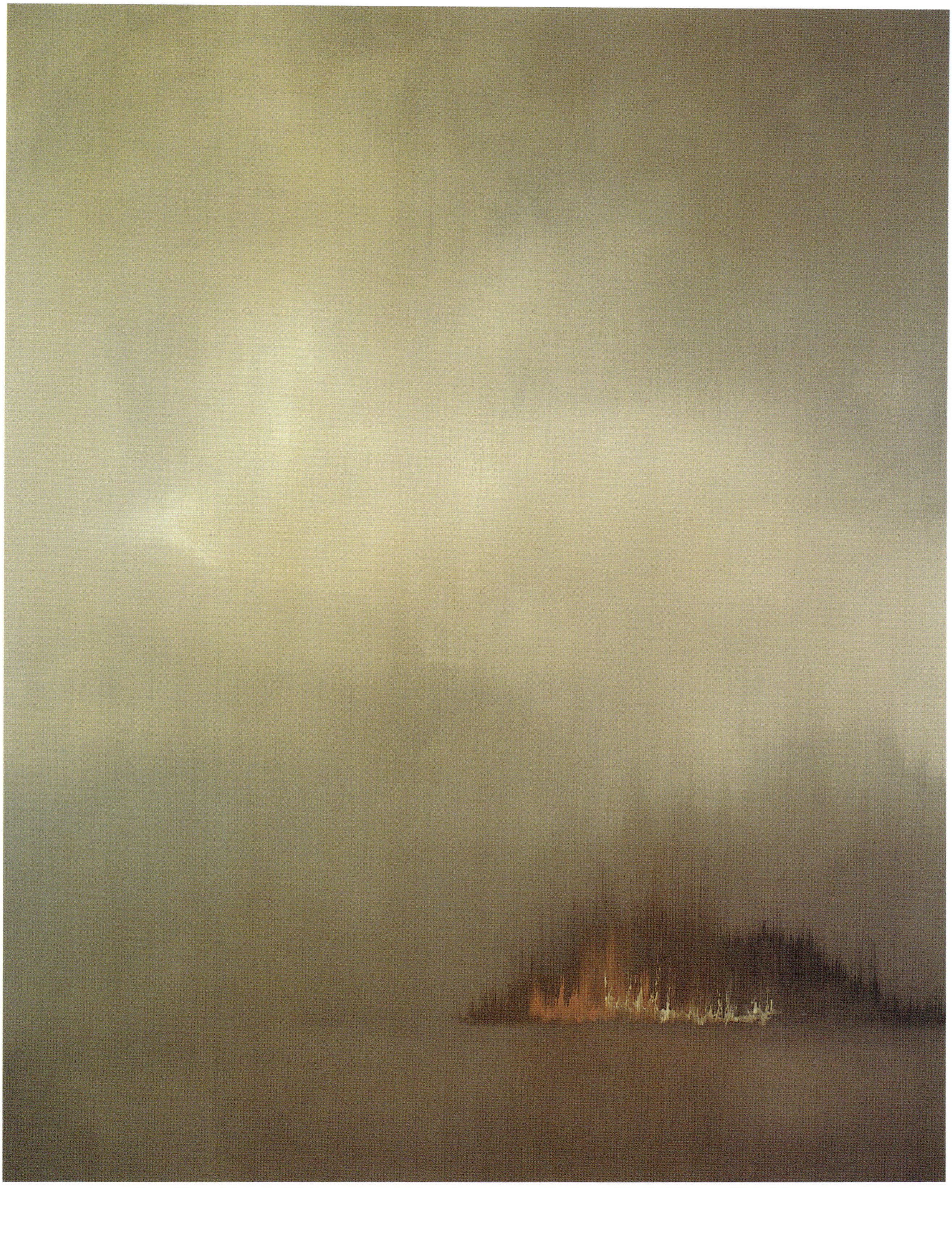

On seeing Ann's paintings, Julian Levi concluded that her best course was simply to stay home and paint. The class was not where she belonged. He proposed that once a week she bring in a painting. They could have coffee, he said, and discuss it. As it turned out, they had more coffee than talk about specific paintings. In time she realized that this was his intention. As her instructor he was convinced something personal in her work should be sequestered and allowed to grow: "I think Julian Levi recognized the inner vision that was compelling me to make a thoroughly individual statement in art. He wanted to get close to it, but he didn't want me to lose it."

Technical problems came up in the course of her self-instruction. For answers, Ann did research. She needed to know more about grounds, stable pigments and varnishes. In a combination of trial and error, discovery of theory and its practical application, she found her own kind of working method.

"In the sixties I went through the traditional method of buying unprimed linen and preparing it—boiling up rabbit-skin glue, sanding and priming with white lead. It was endless. I spent more time preparing the canvases than I did painting, all because I could not find a commercial canvas which, for my purposes, was smooth yet still had enough tooth to hold the paint. There is a quality of surface that is very important for the kind of brushwork I do. When I primed my own canvases, I got that."

She took no more studio classes, but instead, art history. It was important to learn something about the art of the past. But for Ann the more important need was to learn an aesthetic language not available in books, nor in words even, only in painting: "One of the difficulties in learning about art is that reading and writing are not substitutes for the visual impact of pictures." Later, after she began exhibiting her work, critics found in it a likeness to that of Joseph Mallord Turner. As with many things Ann learned, this became for her a matter of learning in reverse. Because of what was said of him, she wanted to investigate his art: "One of the reviewers said that my paintings made him think of the late pastoral Turner. Many critics assumed that I had been directly influenced by studying Turner's work. Actually it was the other way around. Without much background in art history at the time, I did not know who Turner was. So I had to find out. There are connections between my work and the work of past artists, but they are after the fact, not deliberate connections. Although by now I have absorbed much art history, my work is not related stylistically to any particular movement. It is consciously separate."

Ann continued to paint on her own, a process more like working with occasional benefit of coach than like going to class and working with an instructor. But with work the painting grew easier; the technical problems were eventually solved. Ann found it possible to produce a smooth canvas with no

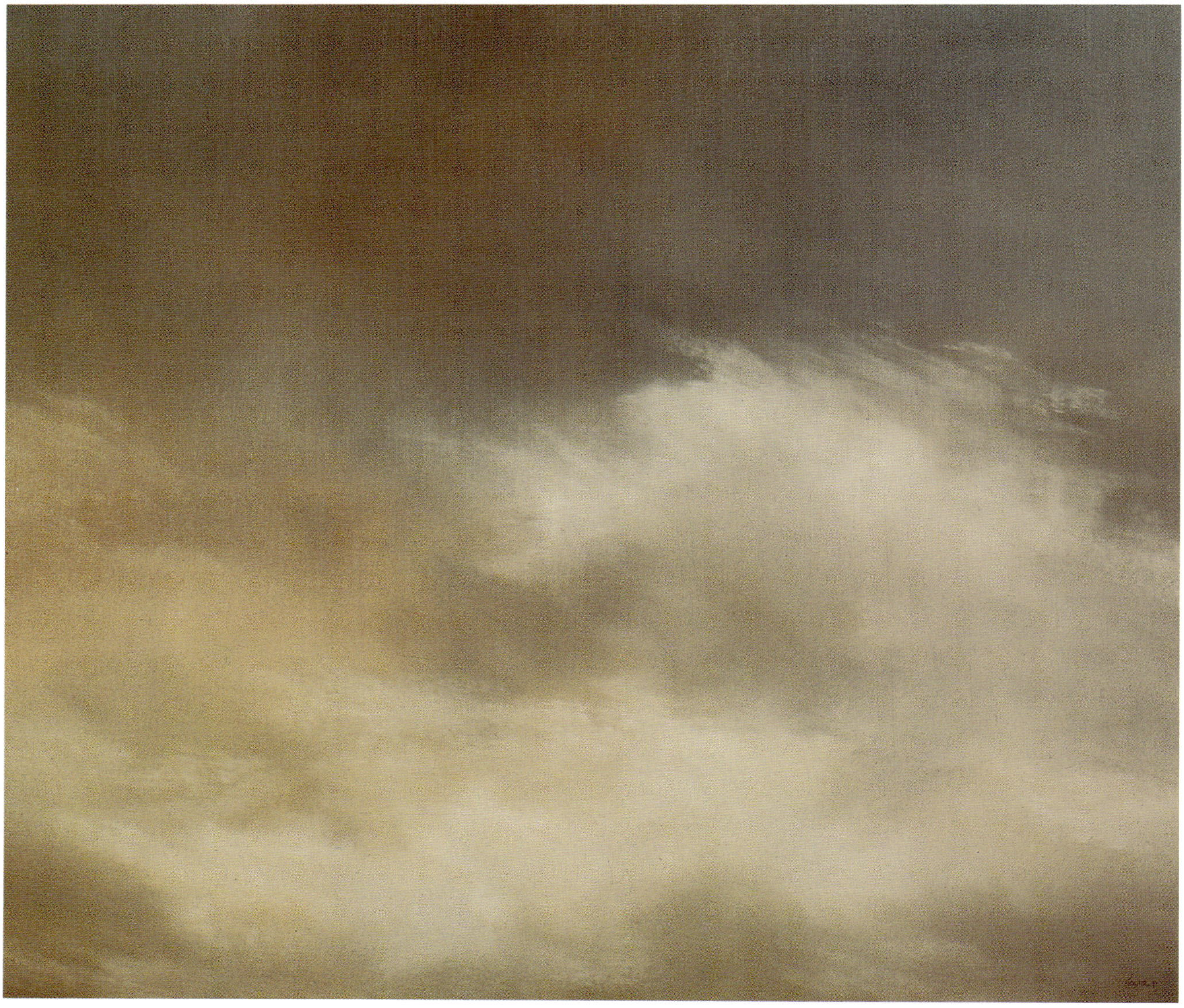

Windward 1971
32″ by 38″
oil on canvas

visible brushmarks. The color scheme was severely restricted, but of the few colors used each had wide modulations. Almost always there were clouds, a source of illumination and, above all, mood.

Windward is a pure example, an essence of sky alone. All cloud, it has few boundaries, like actual vapor in the air. Light, diffused throughout the painting, is its central theme. No literal representation of the sun is there, but its presence is apparent: "The sky has infinite formations; it can be used to portray many formal or atmospheric effects. The resulting paintings can be quite abstract. In **Windward** I made use of a technique I had worked out in **Island.** Impasto paint was put on the surface over the initial, thin coat of wash. Then I drew a dry brush through it so that the edges of cloud were delineated with thicker paint. It gives the illusion that actual sunlight is emanating from the canvas."

Although it was painted much later, **Break** reveals a similar fascination with the effects of light. The canvas is entirely filled with a feathery spread of clouds pierced by sunlight. The greatest fidelity to nature in this painting comes from a believable sense of atmosphere. The space seems moist, as if it would distill drops on your nose. Atoms move in it and form water crystals which fall down as rain. It allows the play of wind. The observer feels the breath of the approaching storm. In other words, it is a realistic painting, reminiscent of Winslow Homer's grand views of the sky, loaded with wind and water, over the Maine Coast or the Gulf Stream. But, as in all Taylor landscapes, in spite of its sweep and coloration this scene is not a real one, however real it seems.

The source of light is placed low in the sky to allow the compositional focus of the work to center there. The alignment of the clouds and the centrifugal force they generate keeps the painting in its designated frame.

Beneath this seemingly straightforward scheme, allowance is made for mood. This has nothing to do with the mechanical requirements of placement. The view, somber and objective like those of the great New Englander, sweeps everything but the essentials out. What remains is limited to the elements of sky and sea and, above all, light. It is as if the infinite drama of the elements was staged in the finite window of the picture space.

In Homer and in another lone giant in American art, Thomas Eakins, the conviction of experience truly recorded became a force. In Taylor's canvases, by contrast, experience is evoked.

Break 1977
36″ by 30″
oil on canvas

Her work is actually quite close to the Tonalists in mood and coloration. These painters, active in the last quarter of the nineteenth century and the beginning quarter of this one, sought out misty hues and pearly, veiled ones. They chose to paint in early morning or at dusk when the record of time is unclear and the contours flee in the half-light. Not the broad colors of the day, but the iridescence of soft light, intrigued them. They selected palettes that rejected the brilliance of the Impressionists' colored shadows. Like Whistler, they summed up the scene before them by means of abstracted shapes rather than by building from the motley world around them thus allowing an infinity of deletion in the name of art. With these requirements, Ann Taylor's work is in accord.

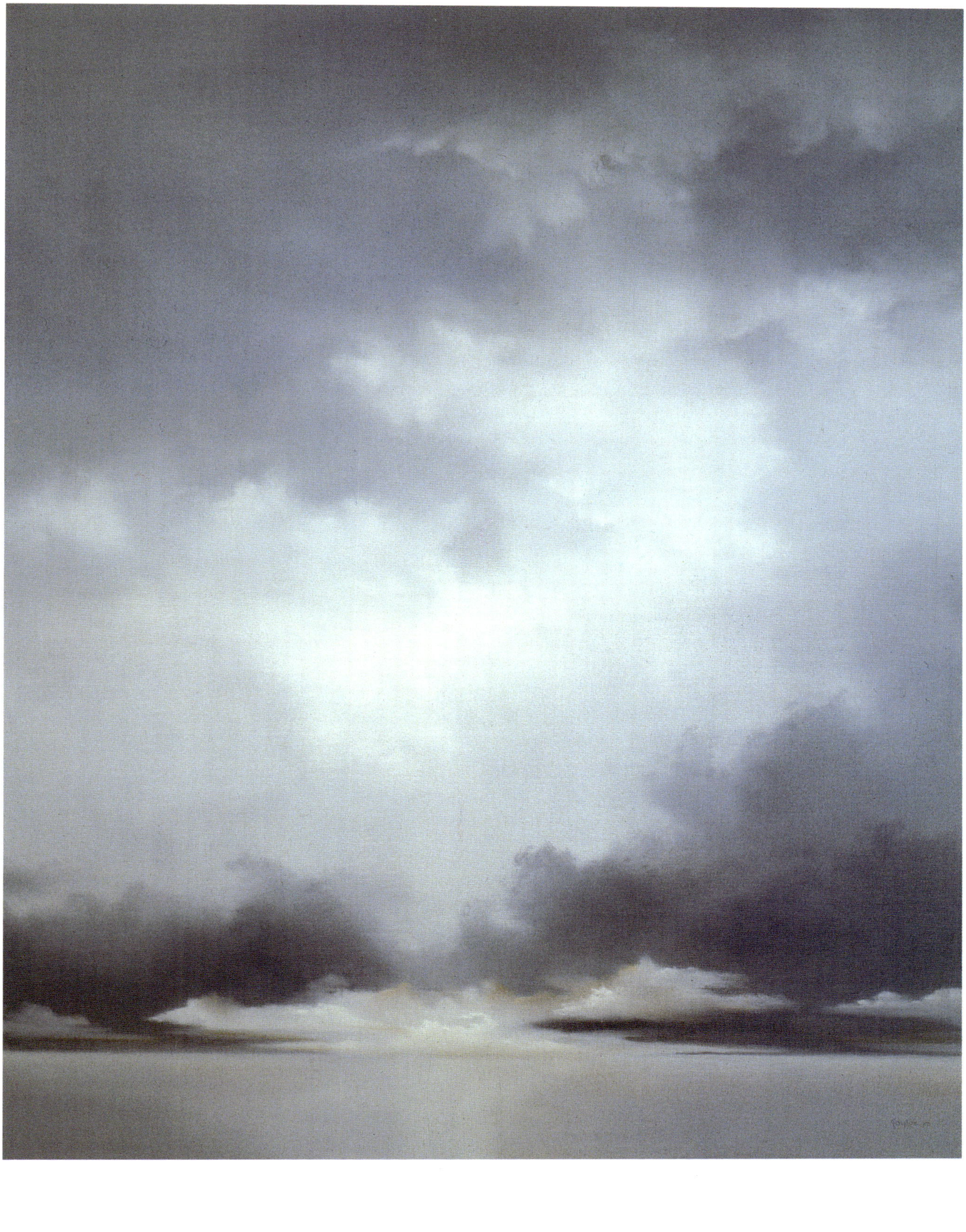

Probably best known of the group, and now credited as its founding father, is George Inness. To him, what mattered in a work of art was the emotion it awoke. Details, he insisted, must be limited to the absolute essentials necessary for identity. Taylor's basic likeness with this point of view lies in the insistence on elimination of detail, on the selection of given colors and shapes.

The qualifying difference is in Inness' criterion of emotion as the primary goal. To Ann Taylor, what is in the heart should be subordinate to the goal of awakening what is in the head. Many Tonalist paintings, even so, convey a mood and style similar to the cloud paintings like **Break.** The scenes are veiled and softly edged; nothing is spelled out.

In the first years Ann lived in New York, while painting steadily and going to school at night, she still found time to see the major art in the important museums of the city. Enlightening though this exposure was, the experience remained separate from her life in the studio. Her studios themselves varied with her needs: a vacant gallery on the Lower East Side, a large upstairs room on Broadway in the garment district, a windowless basement on Bleecker Street and finally a loft at Union Square. All of these working spaces were sealed off from the sky. Nothing distracted her from the expression of her internal thoughts.

This life, full as it was, had its light side too. After classes, students went on to the White Horse Tavern and spent hours in the traditional way, philosophizing over tankards of dark ale. It was there that Ann met Peter Wendt, a German-born designer working for an engineering company. Like interests and like curiosities drew them together. In a short time they discovered they could live harmoniously and in 1963 they were married.

All the while it was necessary, too, to earn a living: "I worked at all kinds of jobs. If I could manage it, I worked only half a week and painted the other half. For a time I made stage sets and costumes for a puppeteer company. This was quite fun, except for the pay, which was awful—a dollar an hour! One of the most fascinating jobs was with a fashion photographer. I was the person who did everything except push the shutter: the sets, some of the styling, the darkroom work. It was alive and I loved it. Working with those frenetic people counterbalanced the quiet of painting alone in my studio. Of course it also augmented our finances until I began exhibiting and selling paintings."

As the number of completed paintings grew, another factor appeared: Ann realized that painting only for herself was not fully satisfying. From the outset she had been sure art was meant to be communicated. Exhibition, allowing her work to reach other people, would accomplish that. She could never have imagined, however, the sequence of events which resulted in her first exhibition, a story which "seemed like a fairytale" the way it finally took place.

The story began with the fact that a college schoolmate had bought a painting. By a chain of familial circumstances it ended up on the walls of Ann's aunt and uncle, Pinney and Dick Deupree, who lived in Cincinnati. As collectors, they were having a party to celebrate the unveiling of a different work, one they had bought from a Cincinnati dealer named Carl Solway.

Fairytales are known for their simplicity: the artist's magic wish is granted when a dealer sees a painting, asks who did it, seeks out the artist and plans an exhibition. For Ann, that was the way it happened. When Carl Solway came to the party, he saw her painting on the wall, asked who the painter was, went to New York and sought her out. He scheduled her first gallery exhibition in Cincinnati in March of 1964.

Still, in any good story, there is always at least one complication. In this one it was furnished by the weather. The Ohio River flooded and cut off all arteries to the city. Except for a few friends, her family and her husband, Ann's first opening was unattended. She stayed one more day in Cincinnati and returned to New York, having had her first show with no public present.

Nevertheless, the happy ending prevailed. The subsequent success of the show grew gradually clear as the cards and calls from Carl Solway announced that in three weeks thirteen paintings out of the fifteen exhibited were sold. "You are the greatest!" he wrote. It was the beginning of a solid, rewarding relationship.

The moral seemed clear. Ann reasoned that if she could successfully exhibit in Cincinnati, there was no reason to suppose she could not do it in the most important city of all. To exhibit in New York became her goal, although she knew that there, fairytales would have scant room.

That proved to be true. New York was indeed a tougher place to make it. But she was buoyed up by a sense of wonder from the positive response to her first show, a sense still undimmed: "It amazes me that there I was, only a twenty-year-old, and people in their fifties and sixties who were serious collectors looked at my work and liked it well enough to buy and live with it."

In a letter to Ann, Nell Skillin, one of her collectors, wrote, "Your beautiful painting, **Gold Light,** is now hanging against an adobe wall in my room and gives me quiet and inspiration, both. It opens a window to the ocean horizons of my early life first. But then that gold light leads me to the vaster horizons of my maturity—the universe, soul and spirit. Some day, in the long future, you will wonder how, in your youth, you set on canvas the exploration of age. Then you may realize that the gifted person has a very unusual endowment, an inner vision."

The Cincinnati exhibition was a milestone. It brought the fledgling artist a new charge of energy, a conviction. It was a portent, a favoring sign: "After my show with Carl, the possibilities of exhibiting were open and exciting."

Ann's first step in looking for a New York dealer was to visit a woman named Betty Chamberlain, who ran a non-profit organization called the Art Information Center. This, in effect, was a clearing house between artists and dealers. Dealers might come in and look at the slides left by artists, and artists might obtain the names and addresses of dealers.

Betty Chamberlain was careful to keep abreast of the whole gallery scene, to know what kind of work suited which gallery. In that way, she could furnish artists with lists of dealers selected from a basis which took their work into account. Armed with this preparation, they might show their slides to reasonably good purpose, avoiding the hazards of random approach. She provided "a few of the top-line galleries and everything else down the list: uptown, downtown, co-op, and so on. She was a thoughtful, intelligent woman who had the information needed for both sides."

For Ann, it went against the grain to walk into a gallery and show her slides and paintings face to face without an appointment. She found, however, that this method, while contrary to recommended etiquette, resulted in seeing more dealers: "If you tried to make an appointment, you couldn't get in. If you walked in off the street, they had to see you. You were standing right there."

Ann began a regular Saturday procedure of loading up the station wagon with her paintings and starting out to make the rounds: "It was very hard. The response of most directors was to ask how much I had sold. They seemed only interested in the commercial aspect of art. Although nearly all the paintings I exhibited with Carl were sold, that was not enough. They queried me on my non-existent résumé. I was discouraged, but couldn't let myself give up. I needed my paintings to be seen; I needed critical and personal response. I kept hoping to find a dealer who would look at the work itself. Very few were interested."

Betty Chamberlain's list had been covered nearly to the end, where the "Y's" were. Still no real interest. Ann was ready to retreat a step or two and try for another exhibition out of town in order to build up that much requested, still unembodied, résumé. But she had one name left to go and the paintings were already in the car. She decided to finish the job.

The last suggested gallery was the York Gallery on 56th Street between Madison and Park. The owner, Jim York, amiably agreed to come out to the car to see the paintings. He recalls: "We went down a flight of stairs and there we were standing on the street. I had a wonderful time, a marvelous experience. I fell in love with the work. In New York, I hadn't seen such beautiful, consistent paintings anywhere. Ann's paintings were all of that. I found them very exciting. In fact I still own the first painting that I ever saw."

Here was the direct response to the work itself that Ann had sought. It was the start of a long personal association and three annual exhibitions beginning in 1966. On each occasion, if the show was not a sellout at the opening, every painting sold by the end of the season. It was clear to Ann that although this success was to some extent a matter of astute presentation, it was also a result of Jim York's real enthusiasm for the work: "There is a certain kind of relationship between a dealer and an artist that is sometimes quite magical. It happens rarely. Carl was the first premonition of this, Jim York was IT. Some people instantaneously understand my work. Their response is intuitive, like Jim's. Maybe later they will ferret out the more cerebral nuances, maybe not. Jim and I grew to be true friends. He has had a far-reaching influence on my personal life which in turn affects my aesthetic life."

To exhibit and expose her interior view was a testing for Ann as it is for any artist: "Being in a room with your clothes off would be bad enough. Exhibiting is like being in a room with your skin off too. Your most personal ideas are out there on the walls and it can be terrifying. I think it requires nerve, perhaps even courage, to expose these thoughts. It takes courage to have a vision, attempt to translate it onto canvas and put it out there in the public eye. Above all, it takes courage to let it stand on its own without the force of your own personality. (Not to mention the courage to carry on despite one's detractors.)"

In spite of a reluctance to stand exposed in this way, Ann persevered. She wanted exhibition. Countering her reluctance was her conviction that art which remained unseen failed in its primary purpose. Besides this, openings offered a unique drama: "Facing the public and facing yourself reflected in the public eye is a necessary part of sharing your art, even though it is difficult. I love the theatricality of openings, but simultaneous with that performance and that excitement is an uncertainty and a wondering about whether or not the work has validity. Exhibiting is both a delight and a dilemma."

Like a diver who knows the water will receive him safely but flinches from the shock of its icy chill, Ann braced herself to continue, reminding herself of the meeting with Jim York and his immediate response to the paintings. **Spring Approach One,** for example, had called forth his genuine enthusiasm. Again based on winters in upstate New York, a minimalist view is presented in which snow occupies the lower two-thirds of the picture plane. Above it the color is heightened, the very simple shapes are emphasized. This painting is from the other swing of the pendulum in Ann's work, the defined side where the forms are linear and the distinction between areas of color is sharp. Would others, like Jim York, respond at first?

From the start Ann was determined to handle the business side of her career. In the late sixties, encouraged by her successes with two dealers, she initiated a plan designed to secure representation in galleries in other parts of the country, anywhere some interest in contemporary art had surfaced. She wrote to museums in major cities and asked which galleries would be suitable for her work. Armed with names and addresses the museums furnished, she wrote letters enclosing slides and reviews: "I am basically two-headed. One head makes the art; the other manages my career. It is not difficult for me to split like that, but I think it is not expected of an artist (or of a woman for that matter). It has turned out to be both an asset and a battle. Some people who run galleries find it uncomfortable. There is a fundamental division between creators and managers. When a creator can also manage, it may sometimes seem like pulling the rug out from under the manager."

Spring Approach One 1967
8″ by 30″
oil on canvas

It had been seven years since Ann's first quasi-showing—one painting hung as a student of Julian Levi—and in that time her technique had developed and matured. Jim York noted on first seeing her paintings that apart from being very beautiful, they were also technically sound.

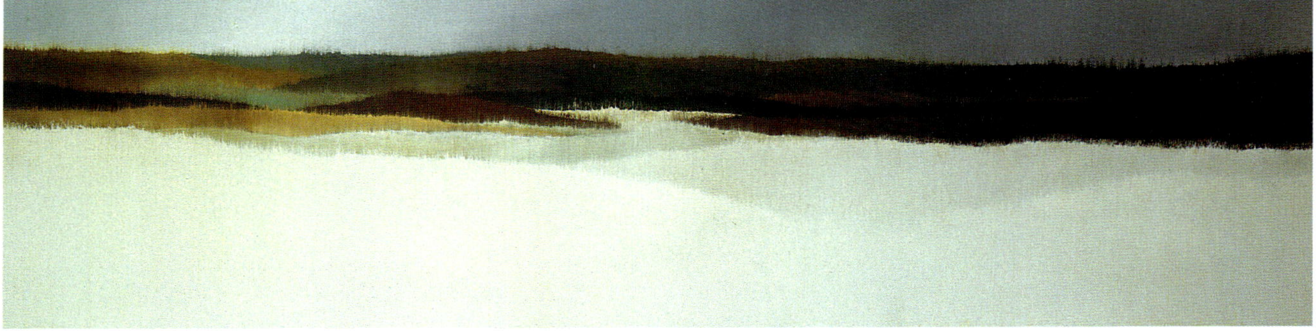

In fact, her methods had become quite consistent. She had learned to create a glass-smooth surface quickly and surely. Unless the painting was very large it could be finished in a single session, in one day. The process gave no room for second thoughts. It had to be almost simultaneous from concept to conclusion. If she wished to rework an idea, she did so on a new canvas. The resulting effect was that the paintings followed one another as serial variations on a single idea: "If I begin with a vast idea, I would rather express it on several canvases than on one. I want to simplify, to treat each important theme separately. Every idea, in a classical sense, should have a format of its own, a theatre of its own. It is that kind of honing down that contributes to making my paintings so direct."

Her technique had limitations but it prevented any worked-over quality and kept the absolute freshness of the impulse which began each painting through to its completion. Alla prima painting, in the Renaissance terminology, painting all at once, described the process: "Working wet into wet is the method I use to create the color modulations that give my work its personal stamp. That necessitates painting with deliberate sureness. Oil dries so much overnight that the colors do not blend as well, if at all, the next day. When it works, it works. When it doesn't, the work is destroyed. Before deciding to keep any particular painting, I live with it for three or four months—longer if I can. Sometimes, after that, the paintings go out to the galleries; sometimes out with the trash."

Distinct from technique, which was similar in all the paintings, was the category of aesthetic emphasis into which they could be divided. The evolution of Ann's work is often cyclical, moving from soft to hard edge, from realistic to abstract. Beside the amorphous, cloud-filled sky paintings and those with defined, nature-based patterning were those with a strongly abstract base. The beginning of this direction can be seen as early as 1967 in **The Mendon Diptych.** Although there is much natural reference in this painting, it primarily emphasizes the division of space, both externally—being divided into two framed panels—and internally.

The Mendon Diptych 1967
46" by 60" overall
oil on canvas

Across the naturally horizontal bands of the mountains it depicts, the vertical division is arbitrary, creating two slightly different rectangular planes. The observed pattern of the hills becomes a series of variations on the triangle. Although it derives from land forms, the growth in the foothills, the high Alaskan peaks, the image as a whole deals finally with the repetition of this geometric shape. In the foreground, the lower, more distinct, hills and their reflections create a spiraling concentric vortex. The movement is carried back into the picture plane as the hills themselves recede, achieving a variety of spatial perceptions.

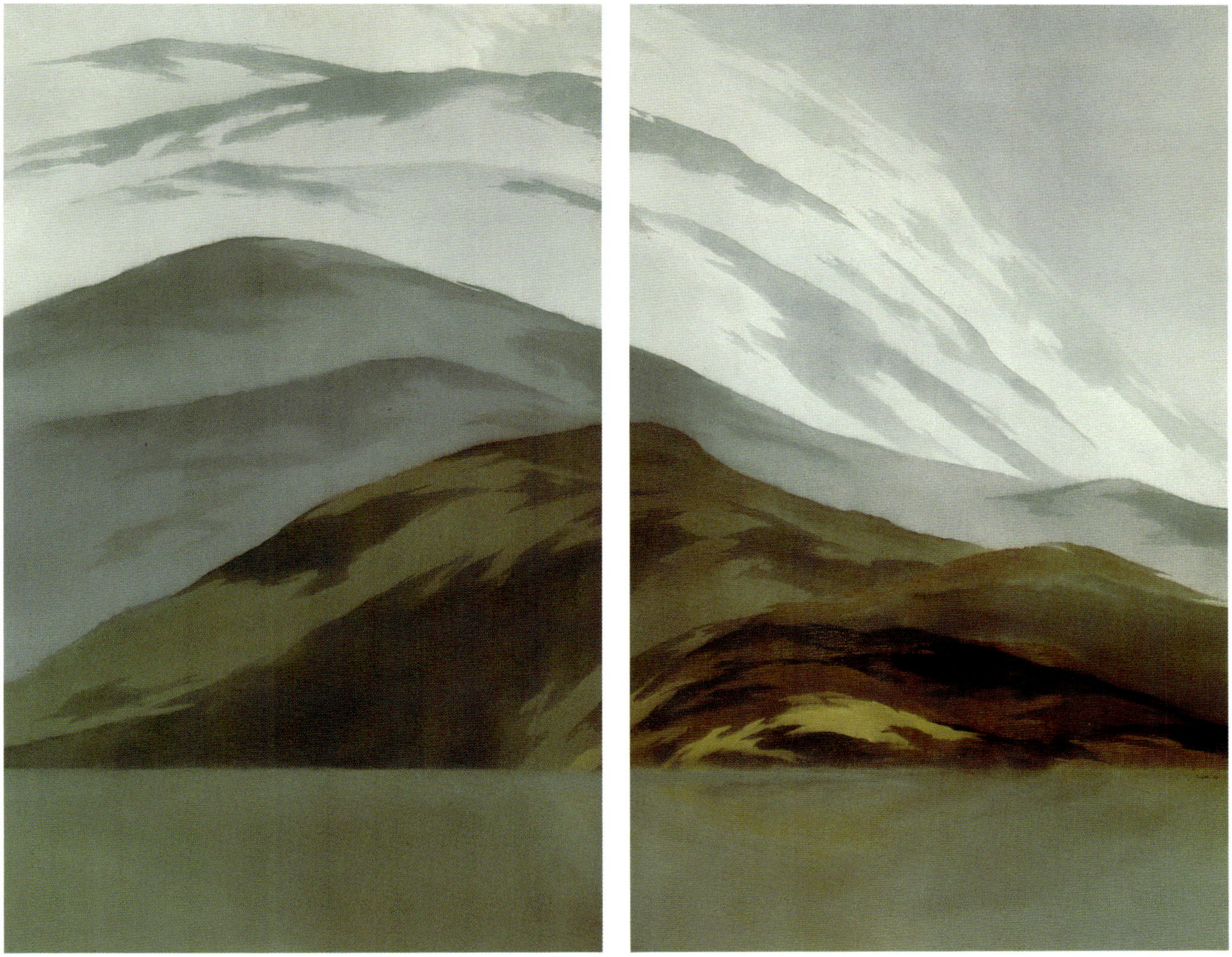

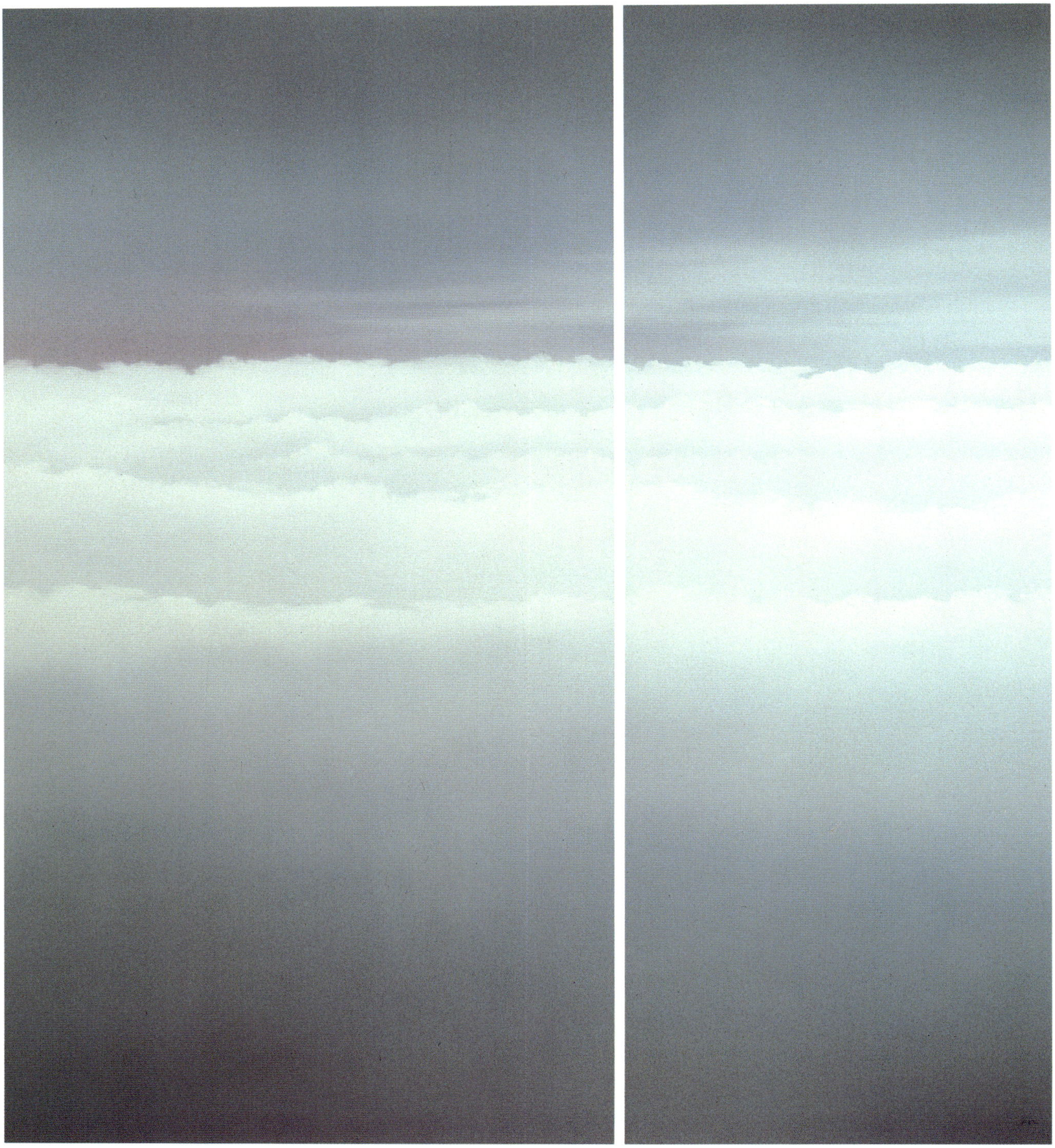

Off-Center Diptych 1973
52″ by 48″ overall
oil on canvas

Diptychs and triptychs serve a useful practical purpose: the paintings can be separated into sections for shipping. But they also serve an aesthetic function, a design function. **Off-Center Diptych** precisely exemplifies this point. It consists of horizontal color bands which nevertheless are more clearly figurative than they are concrete patches of color in themselves. Yet this figurative reference is only a surface layer. The cranberry tinge which opposes and sets off the basic steel blue imparts a certain feel of color for its own sake. Having gone past the first and obvious similarity to the earth's atmosphere, the observer comes to the artist's imposed distinctive division of space which reads as banked, horizontal layers separated by a geometric cleavage up and down. One has, therefore, within the frame, a division into two unequal parts, and then a further division, so that frames are enclosed within frames: divisions and subdivisions. The panels are unequal because if they were equal, the work would have no point, it would fail to move. Tension between parts is the engine that makes it run, an abstract quality. Still, although the painting is nearly so, it is not an abstraction. It keeps its reference, however general, to the actualities of vapor, clouds and horizon line. Ann considers it stronger than some other paintings in terms of its compositional impact.

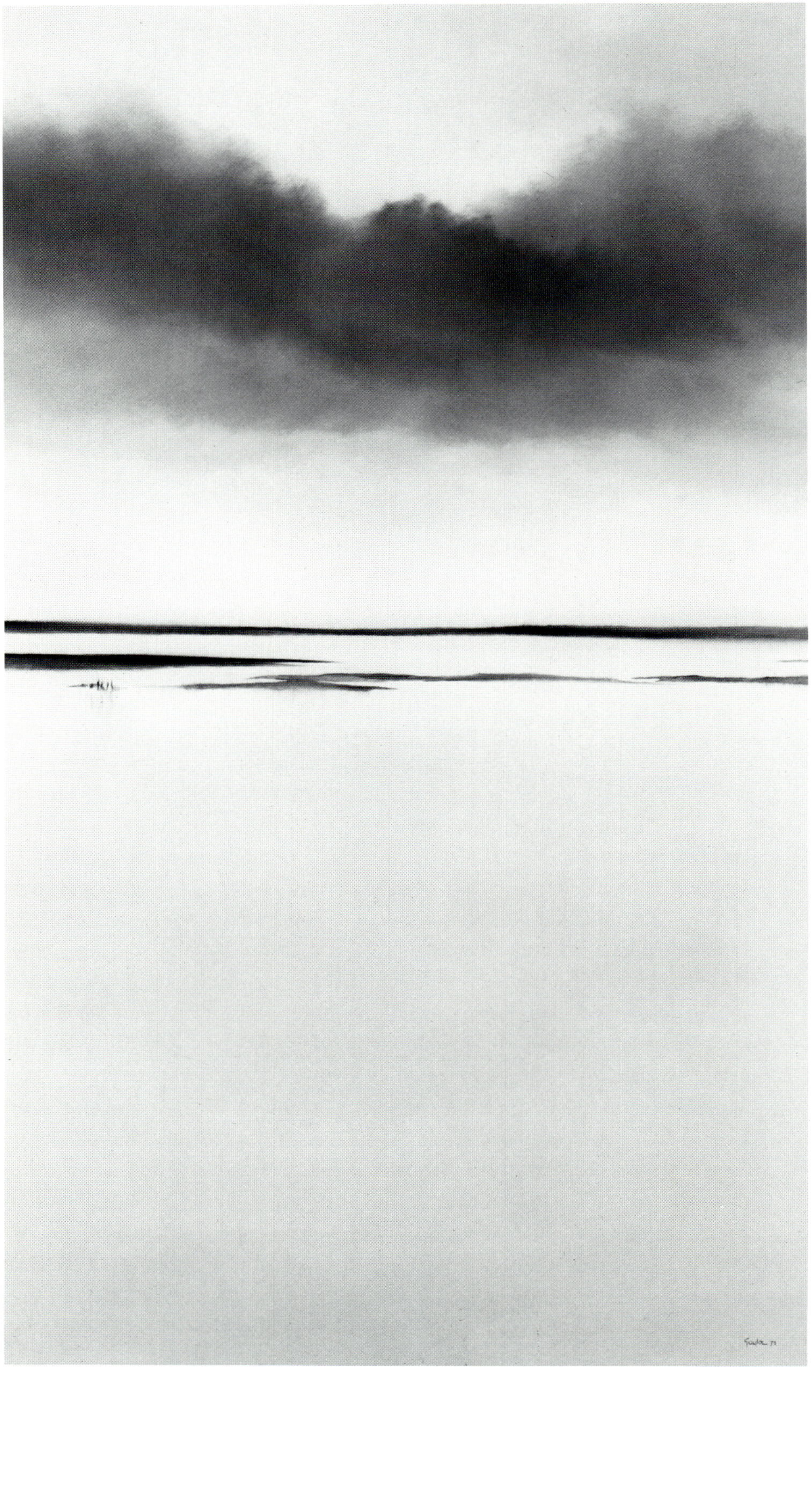

Davy's Gray Marsh 1973
44″ by 26″
oil on canvas

Davy's Gray Marsh provides the same structural ideas in germ: the division of space into square and rectangular shapes. Additionally, it offers an example of the palette derived not from observation of a subject but from a play of variations on a given pigment, in this case Davy's gray. The fact is that the color is actually a given, selected a priori. It is nature as shaped by the artist's organizing eye. **Davy's Gray Marsh** was painted in the same year as **Off-Center Diptych.** Though it appears more representational at first glance, in fact the clouds, the sheets of water in the marsh, bear a resemblance to the divided and subdivided forms in the diptych, an almost replicated patterning. Again, the impulse to abstraction is very strong, but it stops short of departure from experienced images, sifted and shaped though they may be.

The shape theme developed from drawings done in Alaska and on a trip to the Southwest in 1968 appears in Ann's work in different guises: "A number of drawings and paintings derived from my first trip to Alaska, and from my second, eleven years later. On the first trip I took a rice paper sketch book that folded out like an accordion. I had never drawn from nature before. I filled that little book with miniature ink drawings of the mountains, the tundra, the open wild. Later some of the sketches were expanded to full-scale drawings. It was an aesthetic adventure and I loved making them. I also gained confidence in my ability to draw."

Because hers is a style of painting which implies but does not stress line, it was hard for her to know the extent of her drawing ability. It was a question which had lain at the back of her mind unanswered: "At some point in the late sixties I felt uncomfortable because I thought I didn't know how to draw. Drawing, I understood, is an essential tool for any artist. So, almost secretly by myself, I got pencil and paper and started drawing things. I discovered that I could render perfectly well. The series of drawings done in Alaska and later on other trips turned out to be more than renderings. **Miller Canyon** is, in fact, an elaboration of an on-site sketch made at the canyon itself in southern Arizona." The drawings, begun on location and reworked in the studio, were unique in that they were taken more directly from nature than any of her other work.

Miller Canyon 1972
20" by 16"
ink on hosho paper

Miller Canyon, executed in a brushy, emotive fashion, stresses the three-dimensional impact of massive walls of rock and the mottled mantle of forest growth. At an opposite pole from the atmospheric quality in some of her paintings, it reveals a sensitive and highly expressionistic drawing line. It is, in fact, "coloristic," lacking actual hue but supplying many gradations through varied thickness and through strong contrasts between heavily inked spaces and stark white. Later, when Ann approached her first lithographs, this command of drawing came to the fore. But in the interim she let it rest.

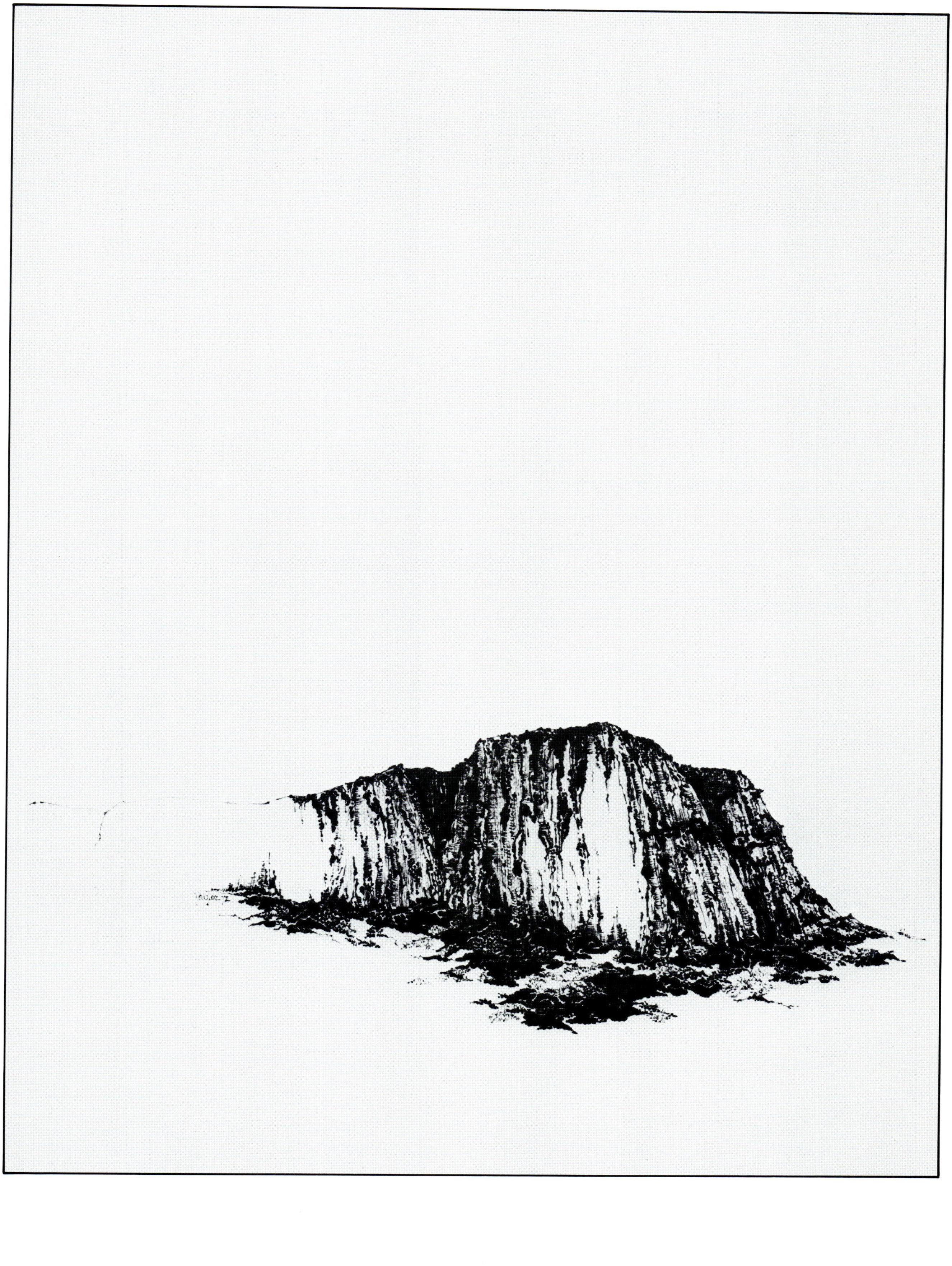

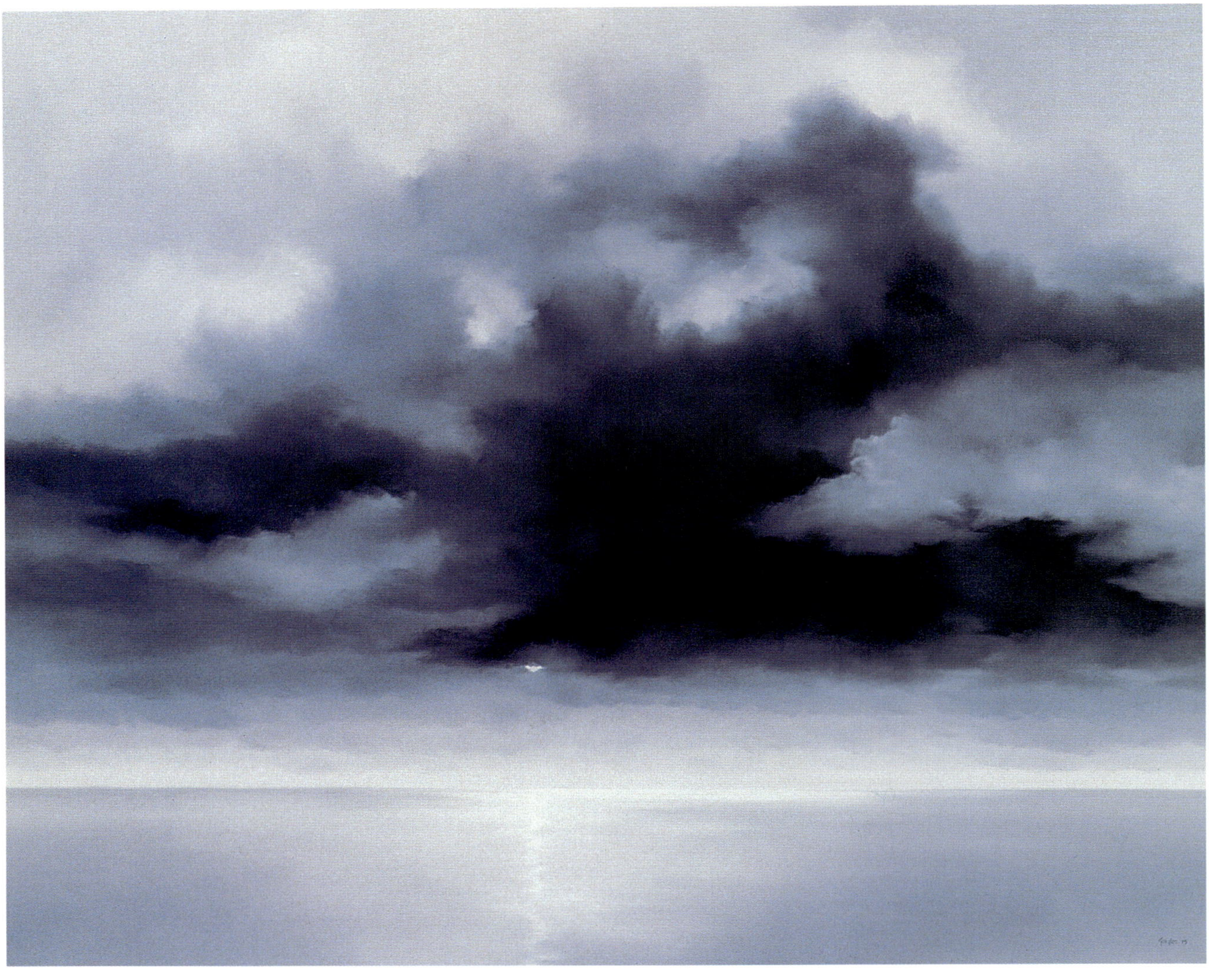

Second Break 1975
40″ by 50″
oil on canvas

The concern for repeated shapes excerpted from clouds, hills and shorelines continued in her painting. Through repetition, from whatever nominal subject, she sought an underlying compositional harmony to bind the painting. These repeated shapes strengthened the design. **Second Break** is not a cloud painting but a contemplation of clouds, a reordering of the sky into a design of rectangular bands and triangular overlays. Art, after all, reorders nature into elements of color and form. Thus, the distant horizon, the light behind the clouds, even the peaks and valleys of suspended water vapor, offer an unending, multitudinous sea of compositional possibilities, wider even than the sea the painting shows. What the artist creates from this is most of all an outer reflection of an inner state.

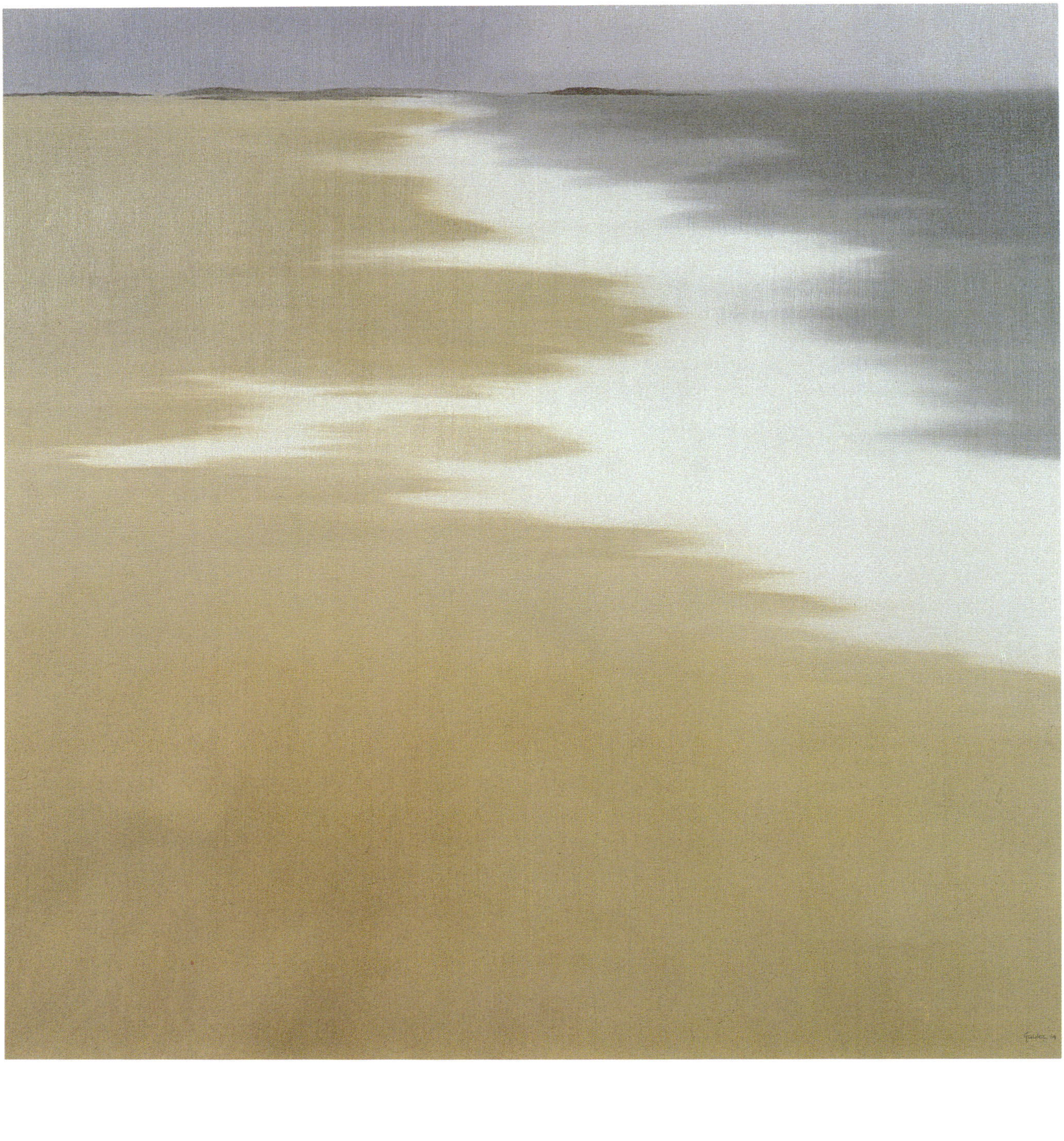

Westerly Limit 1969
36″ by 36″
oil on canvas

In **Westerly Limit,** however, the forms are defined by use of localized color. It is quite plain that the sand on the beach is what it is, and nothing else, and that the line of foam is unmistakably identified. There is no possibility of the observer's interchanging sea and earth. Underneath, even so, the same basic geometric composition makes the grid that holds the painting. The same horizon from a different standpoint is revisited. Patterns from nature are again selected and repeated to reduce the image to its elemental forms, nearly to the point of symbolic imagery. This is a determining aspect of many Taylor paintings.

Ann continued to swing back and forth between the poles of definite line or contour and atmospheric effects. **Umber Mist** exemplifies this progressive dual concern. The strong formal structure—a hard-edged layering of shapes—contrasts with the curling, lingering wisps of mist, which add a dimension of mystery, of aloofness to these solid ridges: "It is possible that this painting shows an influence from the study of oriental theories of art and philosophy I had been doing for several years. About this time I was also interested in Chinese scroll painting and the sumi watercolors. I took a few classes in the technique. The only instruction available was in Chinese flower painting, a lovely art but not one that interested me intensely."

Ann was seeking to express, through space, through the color-filled void and the absence of detail, the macrocosm which is implied. As in oriental art, the immensity of nature in the "floating, fleeting world" need not be stated in detail. Because nature is so vast, a miniature allotment remains to man. The oriental artist suggests; he does not state. More of the head than of the hands, Ann's painting is absent of brushstrokes as well as of details.

The major difference in point of view between Ann Taylor and the oriental artist comes, however, from her insistence that she is painting the type, not the real mountain. However much he distilled essence from reality, the oriental artist had an actual mountain in mind as a start. In her own way, so did Ann, but like Plato, she thought in terms of the ideal world, not the one her eyes beheld. The difference in land forms made its impression on her, nonetheless. It made itself felt in the configurations of the paintings, as for example in **Umber Peaks** (see frontispiece).

This painting speaks of choice over appearance, of the decisions of design. It is not a natural scene. It is a selection of elements reassembled like a mosaic: "The use of generalized forms is a device which presents the land without necessitating reference to a specific place, giving a sense of anyplace. In the case of **Umber Peaks,** that place is somewhat narrowed. The jagged peaks suggest new mountains, not the eroded kind, the colors suggest aridity; the middle height suggests the West, not the Andes or Alaska."

Umber Mist 1971
40″ by 40″
oil on canvas

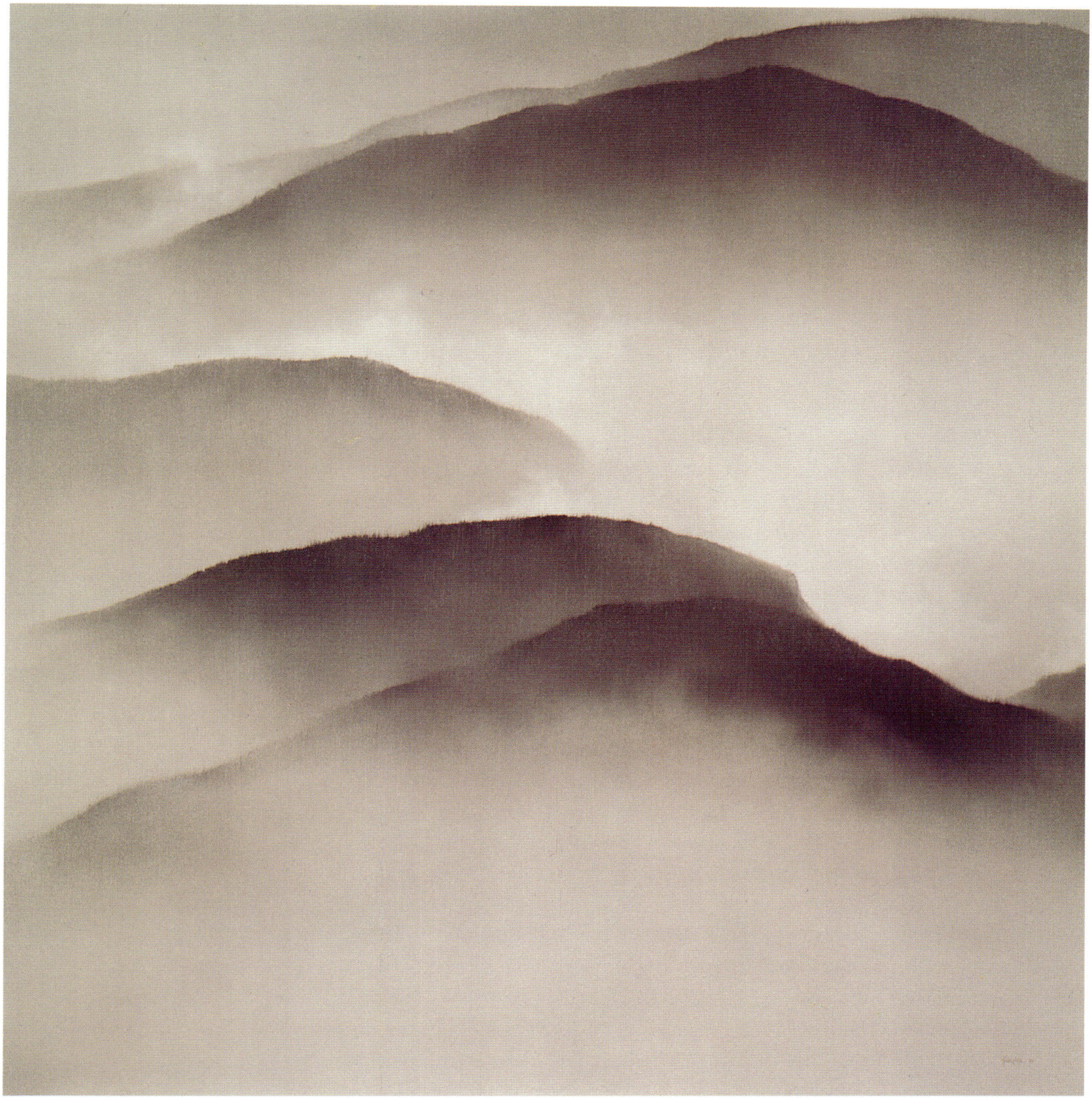

Layers of cloud rise, hiding the natural valley floor. The irregularity of a real range of peaks in haphazard skylines is hinted at, but the color, which is clearly grays shading to blue-blacks like close notes on a scale is schematized, non-naturalistic. The lighting, too, coincides with the form. It is obviously imposed for the purpose of design, progressing as it does from the nacreous lit openness of cloud through the eerily shadowed closer range into full light. As Ann describes it: "The color in these hard-edged mountain paintings simply has no relationship to reality at all. I was intrigued, trying to make the sky almost a complete, flat color that modulates toward a light source. Something mysterious emerges through silhouette and backlighting. There is an ambiguity, a mystery, that is important to the mood of the painting. The ambiguity sustains it."

In the late sixties, Ann's life in New York was busy with painting and exhibiting. Her friend from Vassar days, Libbie Gerry, came to the city to live. She took an apartment across the street from Ann and Peter. The days filled with joint activities for the three of them. Libbie's own apartment soon became more a piano-practice room than an independent home. It was as if, by design, a third responsible adult had entered the lives of Ann and Peter just a year before their daughter, Alyssa, was born in November of 1969.

Of the birth of her daughter, Ann wrote: "What a beautiful experience! Surely, nothing is more intricate or sensitive than a human being. To me, she is sheer delight." Fortunately, at twenty-eight she had already established her career and was able to take the time to participate thoroughly in Alyssa's early development. Ann found pleasure in her growth, and with Libbie's enthusiastic cooperation in the tripartite household, was able to continue her work.

Her painting at this time continued evolving toward the unlimited western horizon. The skies were reminiscent of those giant cloud constructions which previously had constituted entire paintings. In **Division** the mountains appear, sharply edged and steep, unlike the gentle, rolling summits in **Umber Mist.** More than this, the distance has a different feel. Infinitely vast, it opens on an uninterrupted view. The clouds, feathery but banded, extend in atmospheric ranges of their own to the same immeasurable extremes. Distinct from the enclosed, tamed forms of the eroded, eastern peaks, this view of nature opens to the West and whatever wilderness lies out of sight, beyond the mountain range.

Division 1978
46″ by 60″
oil on canvas

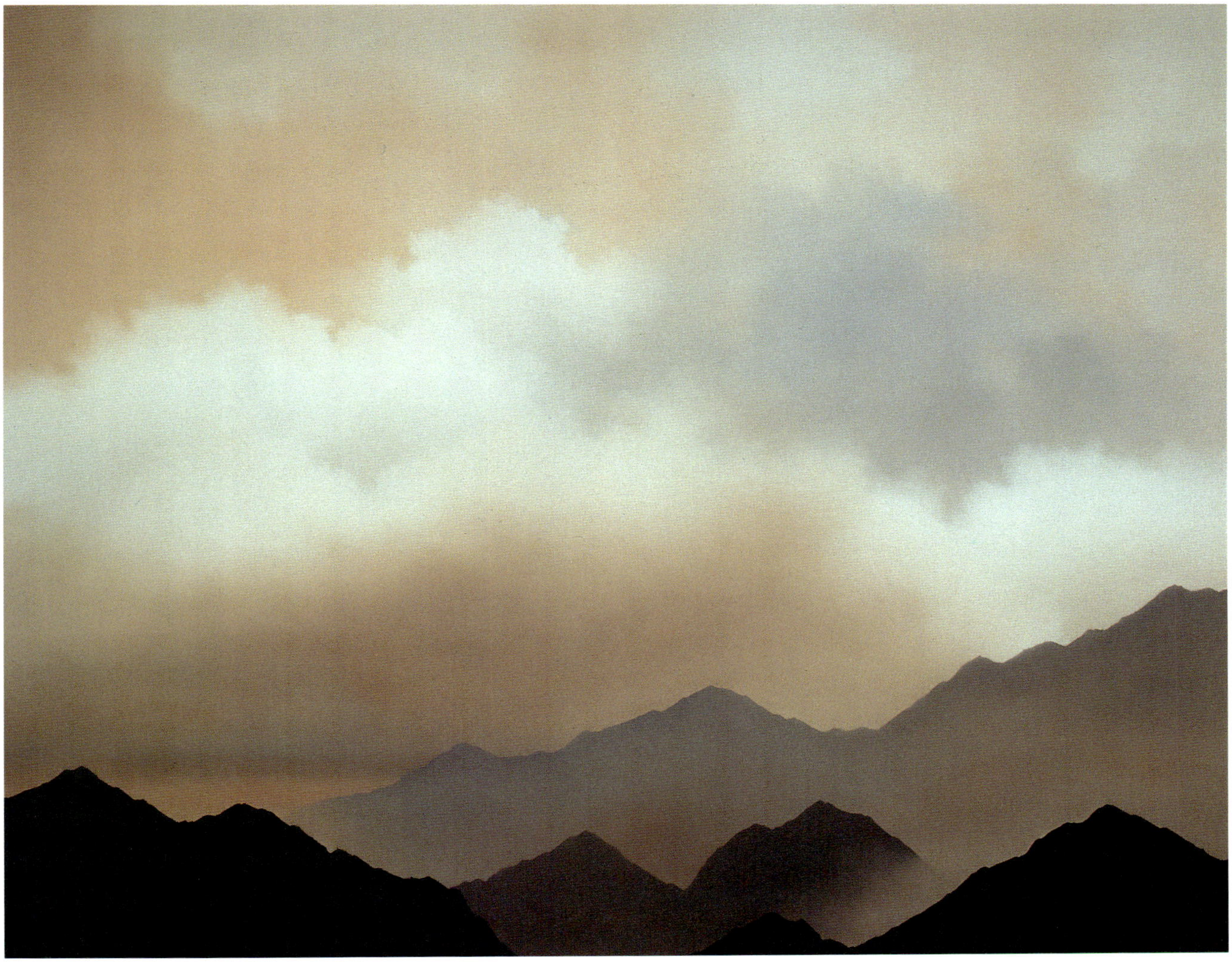

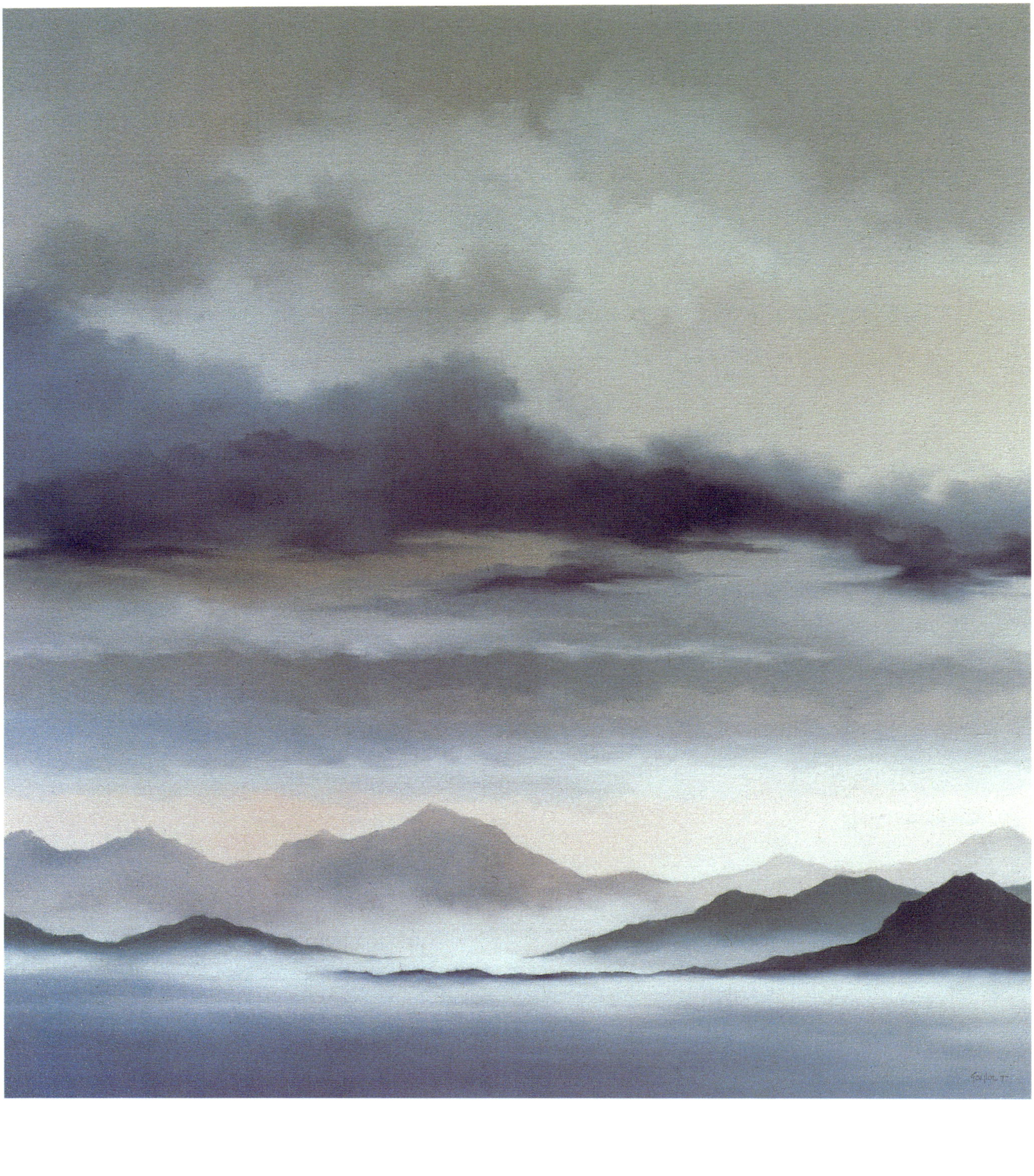

Approach 1977
32″ by 30″
oil on canvas

Approach is a fully developed example of this type. Reiterated shapes, the same triangular formations, appear in mountains and in sky, but their contours are sharply different in character. The ground lines are distinct, the boundaries in the sky are atmospheric and the color scheme is predetermined, a given. Overall, the mood is one of openness and wide distances. In this is to be distinguished the imprint of the West which Ann received and retained after the 1960 trip to San Francisco, the 1968 camping trip to the Southwest and, most especially, the numerous vacations spent in Arizona.

It grew increasingly clear to Ann that, in the face of all this development, no school or trend was a dominant influence on her painting: "My work doesn't fit in any school; it has no close relationship to any special segment of the art world, only to my own life. It evolves and grows, using itself as a catalyst."

A case in point is **Arctic Rise,** an evocation of Alaska. The familiar Alaskan peaks rise, tall and steep, harking back to the patterned slopes of **The Mendon Diptych.** These, almost vertically departing from the flat, reach great snowy heights. The sliver of land that marks the jumping off place refers to still earlier paintings, retracing that first hint of the horizon in the water paintings of the middle sixties: "What often happens is that in looking at the actual world, I seize on things that I think would be interesting to incorporate into the paintings. When new motifs are found, they add fresh material to the fund of images. Throughout my career, themes have been developed and transformed by the introduction of a new point of interest. Distilling land forms seen while traveling and visiting different areas of the country is often a long-drawn-out process worked out in several paintings. I work in series. Ideas generated from some part of a previous painting are combined with these new elements. Further exploration of any given idea is accomplished, not by re-painting but by extending it on another canvas. Often I work on more than one series at a time. The concepts intermingle. Invariably, after five or six variations on an idea, the work has evolved and a new series has begun."

Ann had moved to New York at the age of twenty, expecting to reap the benefits of that city's art community: instruction in art, an education in art history and perhaps an association with other artists. She participated in many art activities but the learning process for her was a private exploration of her craft and vision: "I learned about art by pursuing a direct and basically unswerving interest in becoming a good artist. If you want to be a painter, paint. The knowledge of other people's work is important for reference and comparison, but a personal statement can only be achieved by serious thought and disciplined work. Studying for me meant studying through the act of painting."

Thirteen years had passed in the city. Even in that metropolitan setting, her formative years as an artist had been lived in relative solitude. Nonetheless, those years were invaluable. They produced a self-taught knowledge of the methods of painting, a blossoming career in the galleries and a determined assurance that she would indeed continue to paint until she was "positively ancient."

Arctic Rise 1976
38" by 20"
oil on canvas

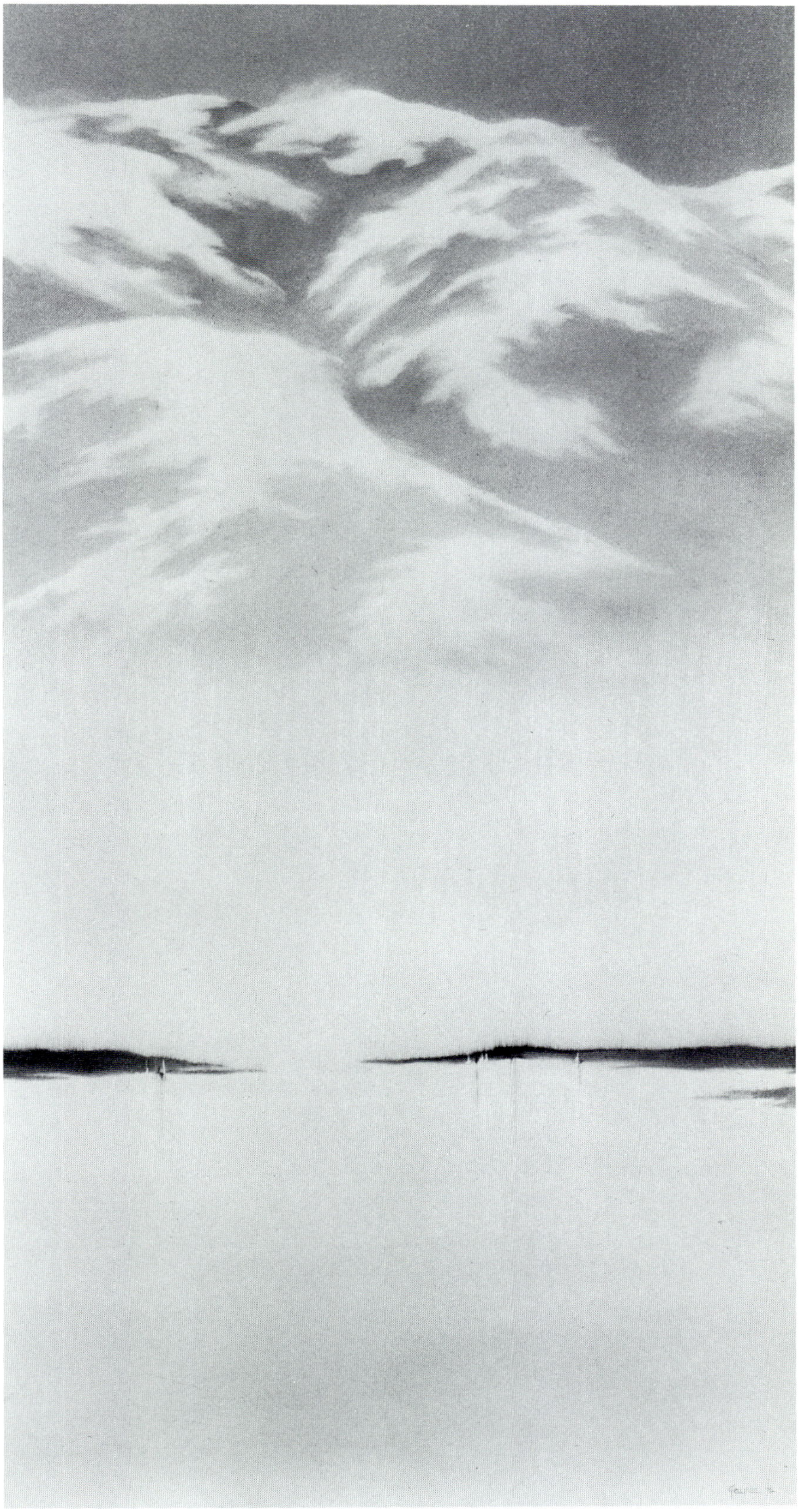

Chapter Three: Beyond the Farther Range

"While I was working on the series in which roads run to the edge of the mountains and then disappear, a close friend of mine remarked, 'I can't wait until you paint what's on the other side!' "

The Hudson River flows through the Hudson Highlands, and these, like the Adirondacks, are old and eroded, offering a gentle appeal. It was from a new home at the center of this romantic landscape, which might have framed itself as a Thomas Cole painting, that Ann first had glimpses of new vistas stretching, it might be, to the other side.

In New York, the horizon line had become increasingly difficult to see. Life in the city had changed in the years Ann lived there. Declining facilities and rising expenses contrasted with the uplifting experiences in the open country of her travels. The need to expand, to challenge new directions prompted a search for land in the country on which to build a house. A large, unsettled tract was found in Garrison, New York, a small town on the river not more than an hour's drive from the city: "It was an extraordinary piece of property, totally wild—a rocky mountaintop with pines which might have been weathered in Japan." The house was carefully planned—an open contemporary design in wood and glass. Upon its completion in 1973, Ann and her family moved away from the crowds and constraints and difficulties of New York.

The countryside in Garrison was remarkable and so was the view from the house. Ann could look down from the height, all the way past the Bear Mountain Bridge: "The river runs deep in the narrow valley. Often, with a change in the weather, there was also an abrupt change in temperature, causing the valley bottom to fill up with fog and mist. It looked like clouds. The light changed constantly within a single day, and the colors with the seasons. It was breathtaking."

The mountains, to Ann, were the déjà vu of dreams newly made actual. Clouds in layers and mountain ranges veiled in mist had already figured in her earlier paintings. Now she was surrounded by them. **Graphic Mountains One** was painted shortly after the move to Garrison. Here, the experience of seeing from the heights, of standing among the peaks above the valleys, of being on top of the world, is condensed, written in imagist shorthand. The pictorial elements are reduced to the very edge of non-objectivity. What remains are only the basic elements: light and the gentle, rolling eastern mountaintops lifting through the light—recollections of the first hillside in Rochester and her later trips to the Adirondacks, the Catskills, the Appalachians. Here is the essence of an Ann Taylor painting, a pattern excerpted from nature, everything extraneous swept away and the clear space a metaphor for the light drenching the forms and colors in the painting: "My paintings are invitations to contemplation. Aerial perspective suspends the viewer in an undefined space. It sets him apart from the scene and offers him a private, meditative state of mind."

The Garrison studio, built from the ground up, was especially tailored to Ann's working practices. It was a large, open space with a fourteen-foot ceiling, a darkroom and vast storage space. A special lighting arrangement was installed. With the knowledge that colors in paintings alter in changing light, Ann equipped this studio with fixtures in which both warm and cool bulbs could be placed. Rheostats controlled them, allowing the room to be filled with simulated incandescent or natural light, or a combination of both, along with a variation of "footcandle" intensity. This system made it possible for Ann to check the colors in her paintings as she worked, noting how they were enriched or drained. Her detailed approach to the technical execution of the work necessitated seeing it in all the varieties of light by which it might later be viewed: "If a building can be perfect, that studio was perfect."

Although the building had one window, Ann covered it with a blind. The views which she had seen in Alaska, the Southwest and now from the high site where she lived, were imprinted on her inner eye: "My work is an interpretation of what I absorb from the landscape." In this way a prototype of her paintings evolved: a model of nature, abstracted, but rooted in real experience.

Graphic Mountains One 1974
40″ by 50″
oil on canvas

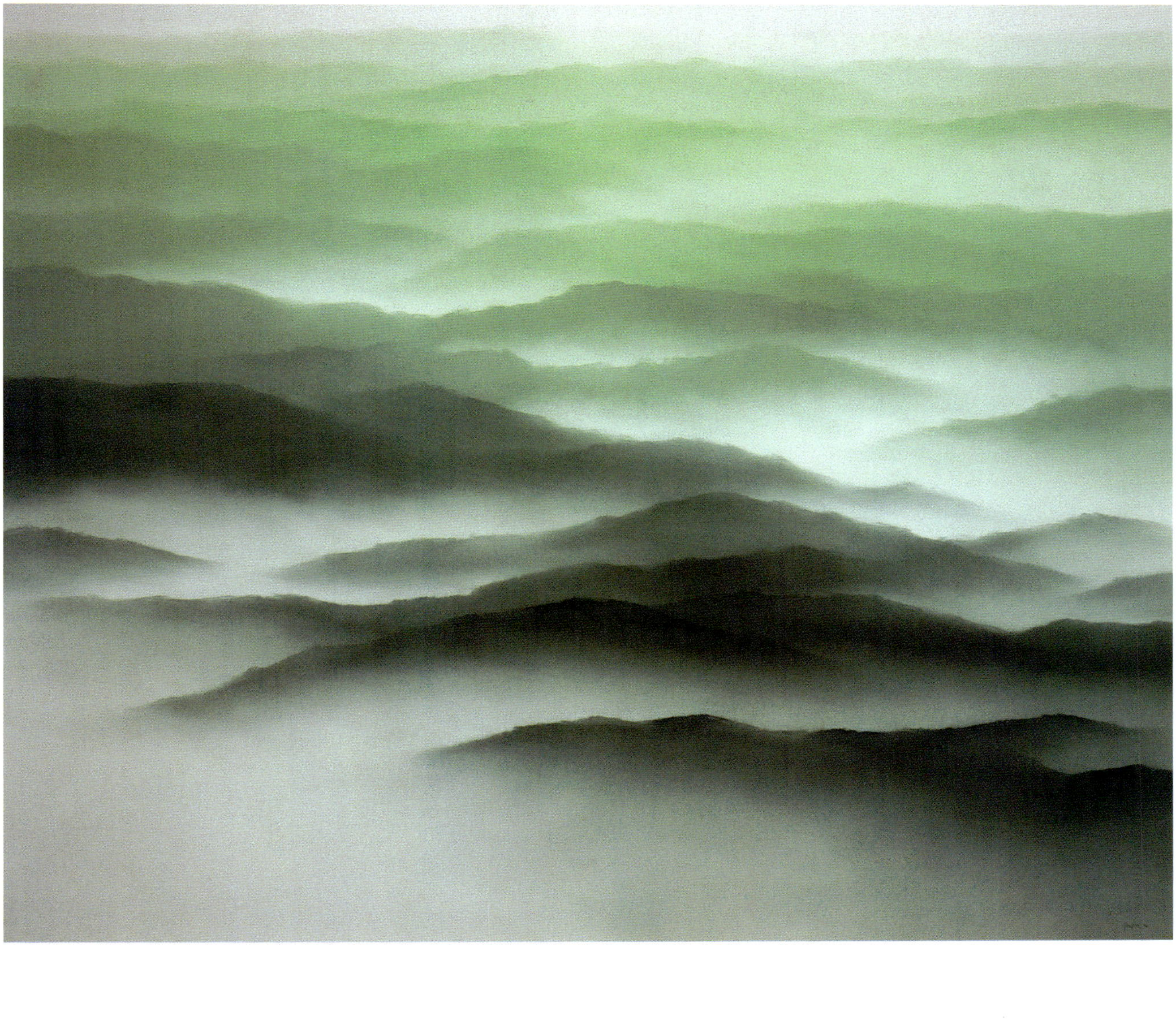

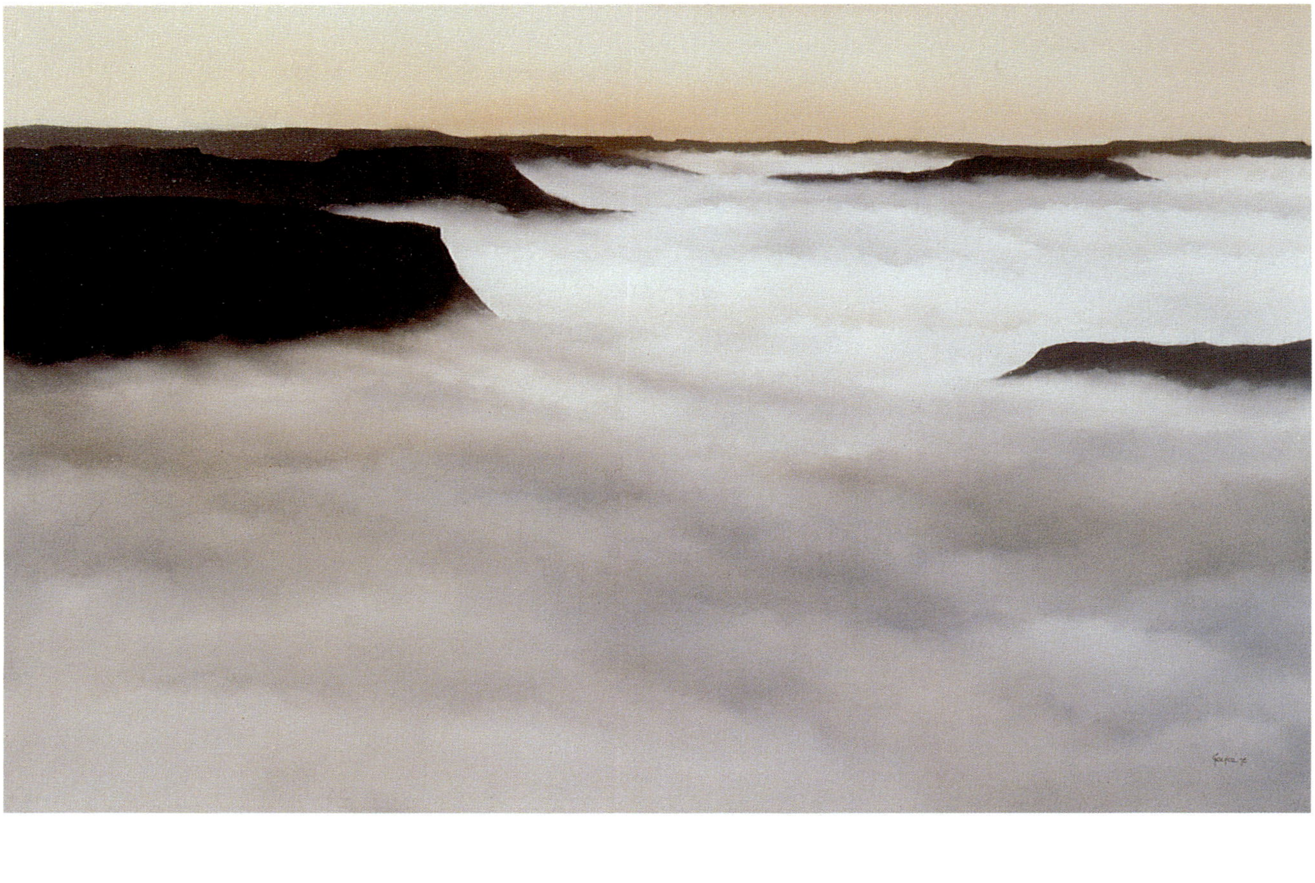

High Mesas 1976
26″ by 42″
oil on canvas

During the late sixties and early seventies, Ann made numerous trips to Arizona. The stark imagery of the Southwest slowly filtered into her artistic consciousness. It was many years before what she had seen in Arizona would begin to appear in the work. Gradually the hard-edged, geometric shapes of the mesas and the southwestern mountains emerged as a foil against which atmospheric effects could be juxtaposed.

High Mesas, in this way, had been experienced without, interpreted within, in the uncluttered, undistracting space of the studio. In the painting, the edges of the mist are as light as milkweed curling against walls of dark, sharply outlined rock. Within their faintly opalescent mass, subtle gradations of pink and rose and peach, the microcosmic rainbow in each suspended water drop, are echoed in stronger tones in the clear sky.

The emphasis is on the experience, not the place. These starkly contoured walls, these cliffs, are not the gentle, rounded slopes of the valley of the Hudson, clothed in green, but the steep faces of canyons in shadow, as if the sunset staining the sky might not penetrate below the tops. An opposition of texture, mist and rock, and an opposition of formal sources makes itself felt. The mist becomes all the mistier by this difference, and the rocks more sharply cut.

A mysterious quality in the painting, a hint of something hidden, surfaces with the depiction of the mesas in silhouette. Ann went on to exploit this aspect in future paintings, especially those with backlit presentation, as for instance in **Winter Promise.** Here, the mesas underneath, dark and impenetrable, are silhouetted against the bank of clouds. Baroque lines of force triangulate the sky and recreate in reverse the angled dip of the mesas' outline. In the major plane of the picture field, the passage of light through swelling storm clouds, the changing illumination, is the main concern. Minimal, however, as the dark foreground is, it is an essential key to the painting. Here is a clear profile, a confirmation of the knowledge of western skylines and the formation of western lands. The cloud shapes are a soft-edged foil for the geometry of the horizon, an interplay of great light-filled expanse against a condensed strip of dark.

Winter Promise 1977
48″ by 40″
oil on canvas

Something of this brilliant, illuminating daylight is present in the views of western cliffs and mesas painted by Maynard Dixon. A major difference, though, is to be found in the structured quality of his canvases which seem, like building blocks, to pile up their sharp-edged vision of the West. His is a hard-eyed view as well, delineated and not evoked, far removed from that last gasp of European Romanticism as typified in the panoramas of Bierstadt and Church. Their grand sweeps of rainbow-filled skies, towering cliffs encased in clouds and, especially, their overstatements were as alien to Dixon as to Taylor.

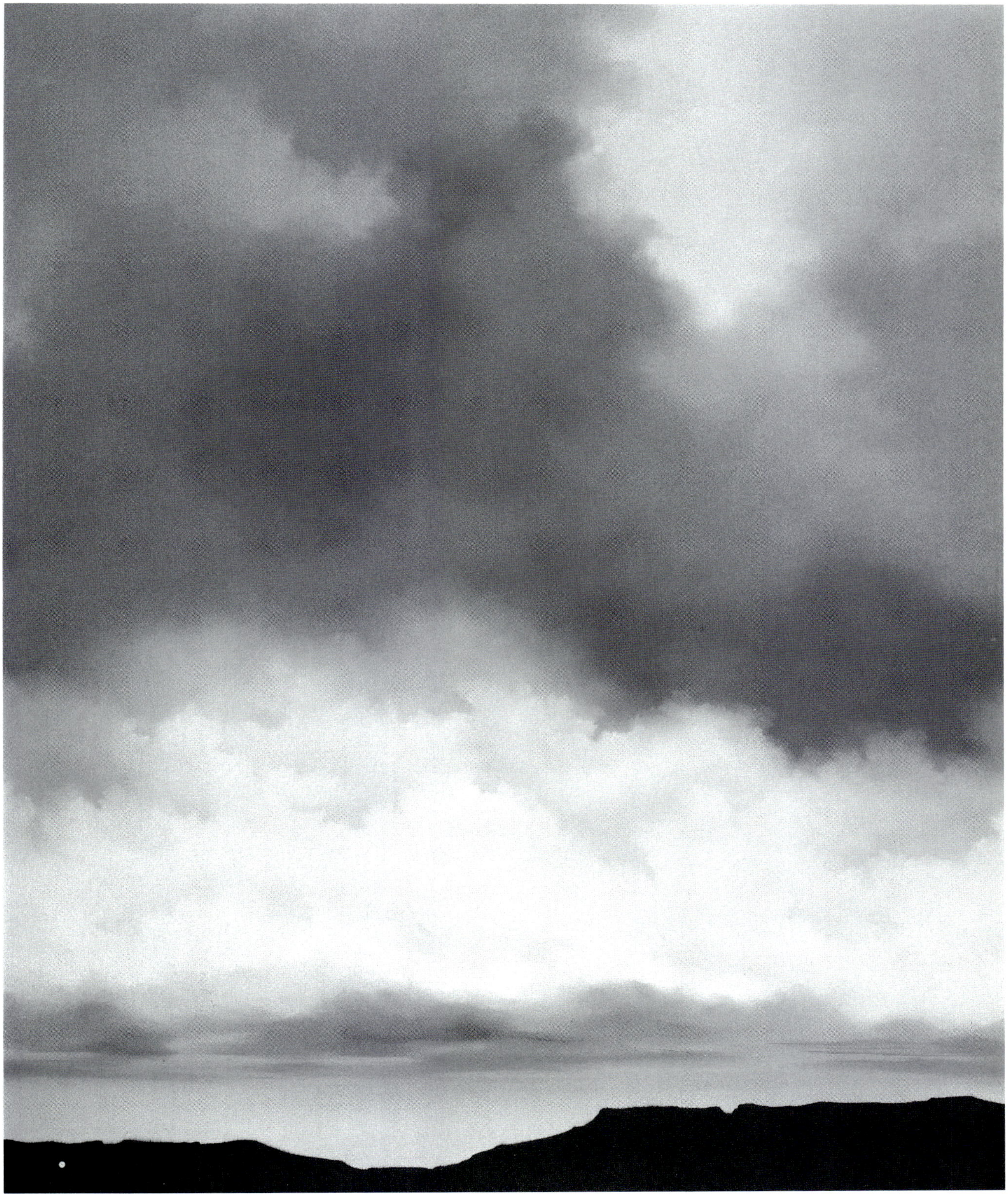

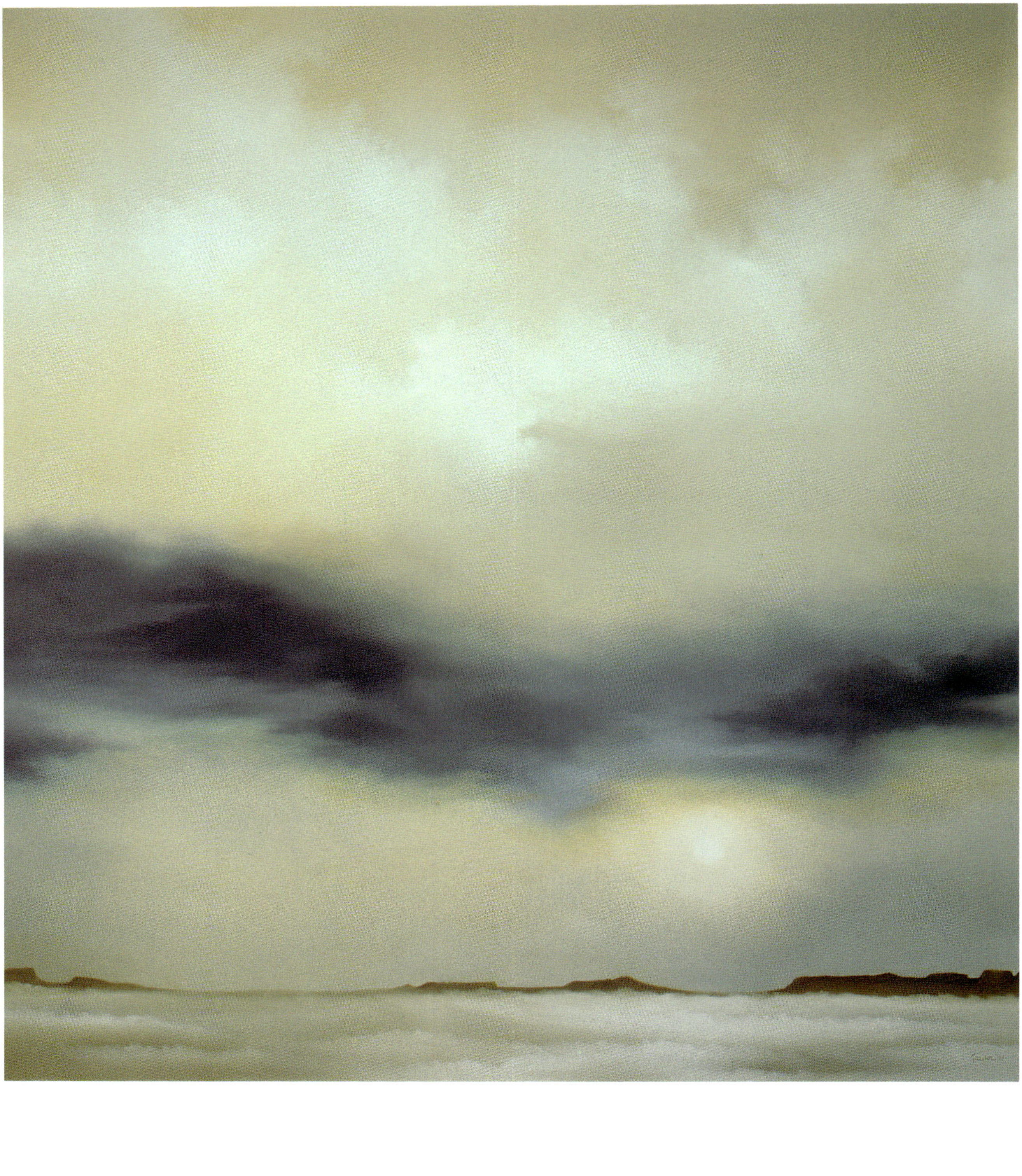

Solar Exposure 1977
38″ by 36″
oil on canvas

Apart from formal structure in Taylor's paintings, and looking beyond likeness to nature, the idea of energy versus non-energy, of matter versus the void, appears to be a consideration. **Solar Exposure,** in this respect, bears a likeness in underlying metaphysics to the framework of thought behind Adolph Gottlieb's "bursts." The stark ochre-brown rim of mesas can be seen as the antithesis of energy, as the void, against which the energizing disc of the sun is played. The major field is reserved to sky, a spatial division like Gottlieb's whose paintings of this type were vaguely streaked along the base with a strip reminiscent of the earth. But his "bursts" avoided figural reference. Their presence is a faint suggestion denoting the separation of sky and earth. The drizzled streamers, as it were, which emanate from the sun's disc, carry the notion of radiating energy with great force. Less schematic, more representational, **Solar Exposure** retains a likeness to nature, but the same opposition of energy to void is invoked.

Ann's concern with concepts of the physical and metaphysical components in painting composition continued in the **Mesa Series. Peach Mesas** forcefully illustrates this point. Southwestern cliffs are staged like actors intruding their play upon the shifting curtains of rising mist. The horizon has moved up the picture plane so that the foreground becomes the dominant feature.

Peach Mesas 1977
34″ by 42″
oil on canvas

To experience this southwestern country fully, as Ann Taylor has done consciously, intensely, on long drives and camping trips, one must be aware from the first of its astonishing clarity of contour. In the clear air you can truly see forever. Landmarks a hundred miles away pop into visual range as if they were situated in some neighboring ranch yard. Yet at the same time there is the shrouding dust, the mirage of heat radiation and, above all, the stereotypical, arid desolation. **Peach Mesas** is dominated by those features.

The famous southwestern photographer, Ansel Adams, insisted on a sharply focused presentation of this same sort of rocky outline. But it is the rich, brooding quality of his images that makes them powerful. Like Ann Taylor, he too is fully aware of at least two "presences" in the southwestern landscape: the physical and the subliminal,

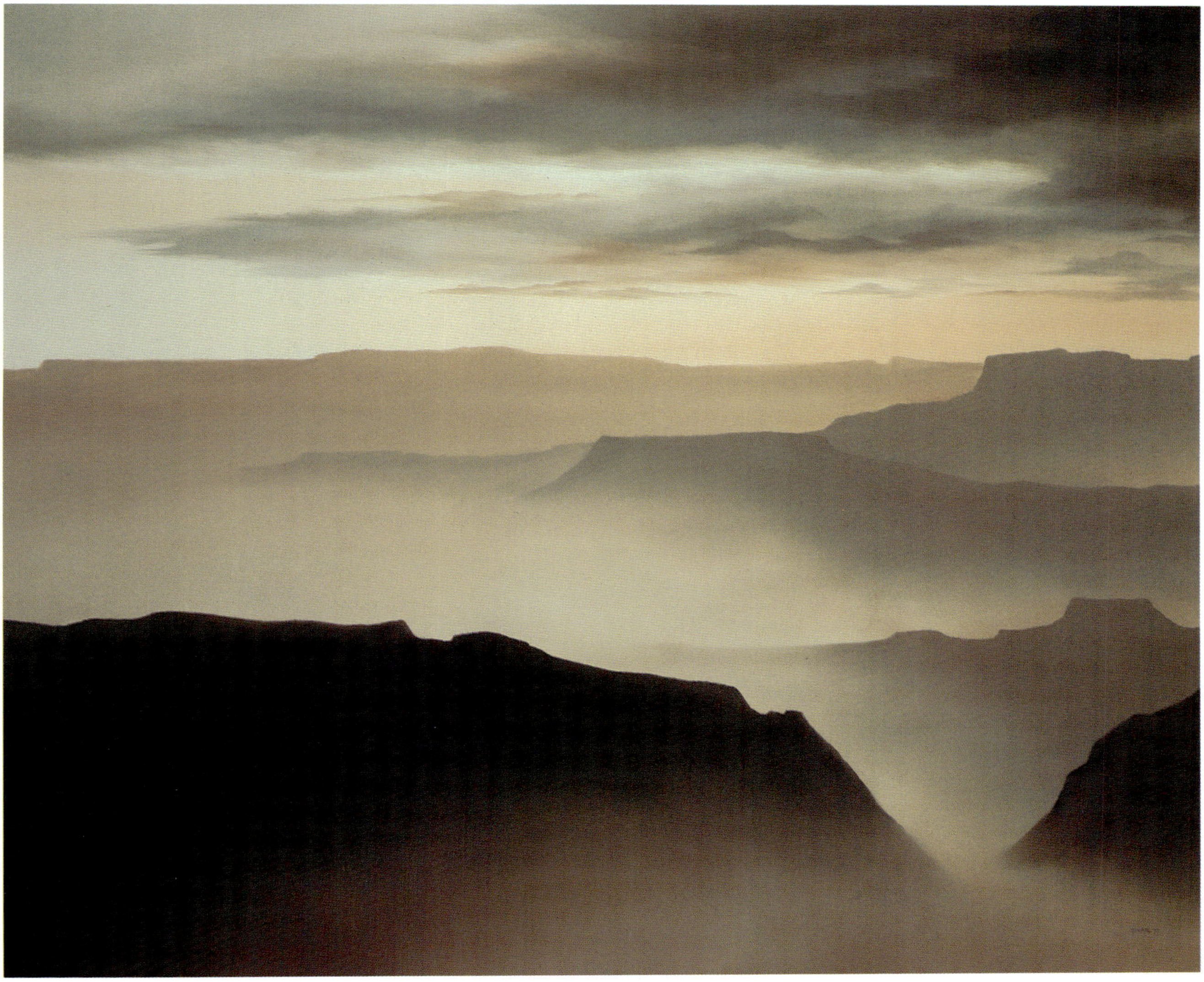

The traveling expeditions themselves in fact consumed only a small part of Ann's time, though their effects were far-reaching and profoundly influential on her imagery. As an artist, she spent as much time as possible in the studio painting or taking care of the business side of her career. The exhibition plans continued. Slides sent to suggested galleries resulted in representation and shows in many large and small cities nationwide: New York, Detroit, Philadelphia, Washington, Rochester, Aspen, Scottsdale, Indianapolis. The number of paintings hung in private homes and corporate collections steadily increased. Press clippings and critical reviews accumulated. With this recognition and a record of sales, the once imaginary résumé had become reality. It was no longer necessary to compensate for its absence. Her career was firmly established.

In contrast to these busy, business-oriented excursions into the urban scramble, there was Garrison—a quiet complement to the unremitting demands of the marketplace. The house there was a shared, even communal, effort. It seemed that balanced living should follow. Solitary contemplation was easy on the heights, but there was a drive, an unceasing rhythm, there as well.

The days at Garrison were short, crowded with country activities—cooking, sewing, gardening—and innumerable unanticipated needs which came with living in a large, independent house. Beautiful as it was, it demanded continual sacrifice of time. Even when finally fixed as plans, schedules did not hold, but changed as the season changed. Ann found herself confronting the renewed acquaintance with nature almost as an antagonist rather than as a friend. Nature exacted a price of eternal vigilance. Living in the country lacked the freedom she had imagined. It was different, but the persistent invasions of her inner detachment, though less immediately apparent than those of the city, were just as real.

The strain began to tell. Like current underneath the surface, the pull of several but opposing motivations in the lives of those who shared this idyllic haven and the increasing needs of the place itself combined to loosen the bonds which held them all together. Their interests developed differently; their paths diverged.

In 1979, testing the idea of again living alone, Ann moved for a season to Arizona with her daughter, Alyssa. She had spent vacations there. She had come to know and use the imagery of the southwestern landscape in her work. Now it seemed that living close to that land might offer the clarity of vision and the contemplative repose she knew was essential for her artistic nourishment.

Once there, her creative energy was released. For some time Ann had wanted to explore other media and she knew several graphic workshops were located in Scottsdale. She contacted one of them and set about learning the process of lithography: "The procedure was very exciting—a completely new language for me. It was an important thing to do. Without assimilating new material, my work could not grow. Invariably any area of investigation would flow back into the mainstream of my painting." It was a concentrated effort: drawing had to be done with crayon rather than brush, colors in lithographic ink did not mix as did those in oil, the image had to be executed in reverse. Finally, however, with her own perseverance and the patience of her collaborators, the first editions of prints were completed.

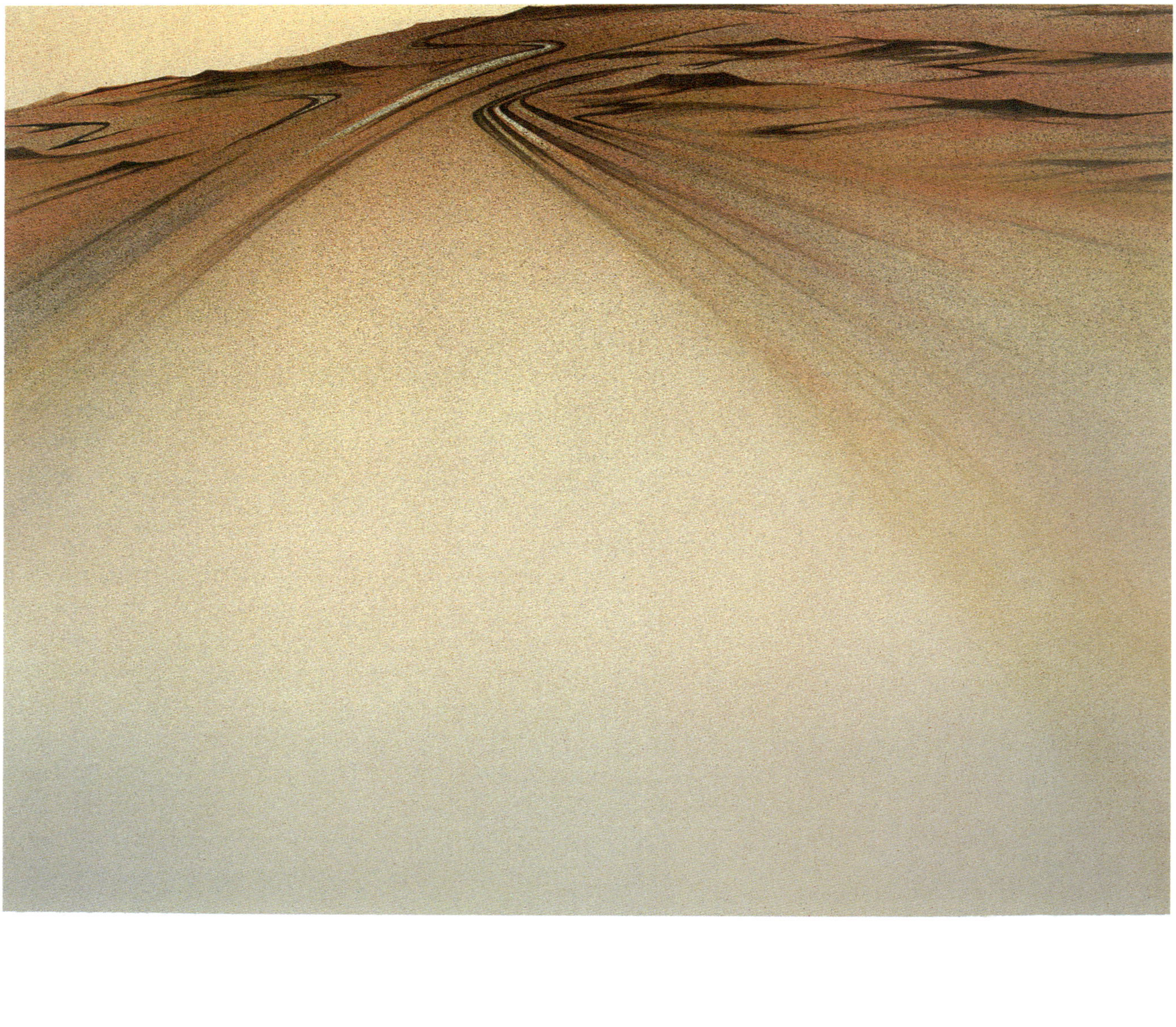

Velocity, done two years after those first experiments, is obviously an accomplished work. It takes advantage of a variety of textures that the medium makes possible. It is an image which combines direct drawing on limestone blocks with airbrush spray. The foreground space is empty, but empty only in the minimalist sense that space itself speaks and, in this case, provides a field for the typical Taylor gradations of color, tone by delicate tone. An impression of movement comes to a point of concentration on the horizon line, tilted like the rotating earth. In a sense, this is a replica of the gyroscope, if it can be imagined as unified with the perception of human movement. As in the Futurists' work, this is an effort to depict the sensation of motion through static visual means. The Futurists portrayed the person or the object as it moved, attempting to suggest the orbit of this motion by repeated representation of the same moving limb or object in different locations. Such a flailing, windmill-like projection assumed a static earth. Ann Taylor too suggests the human side of motion but, in the equation of man versus earth, that constant is changed to suggest the motion of the globe.

Velocity 1981
21" by 27"
lithograph

Simultaneous with her introduction to lithography, Ann experimented for the first time with watercolor. Lacking studio space in which to work in oil, but eager to devote her time outside the lithographic workshop to the production of art, this medium seemed ideal. Despite initial difficulties in controlling the elusive transparency of the pigments, the experiments proved to be beneficial. The watercolors were not ends in themselves. Their different requirements of technique and varied effects would influence her ongoing work in oil as had all her studies in other media.

Life on her own in Arizona came to seem Ann's most likely alternative. When a commission in the East took her back there for a brief period, she reached her final decision: she would formally separate from her husband and settle in the West with her daughter.

There is an interesting parallel here between the lives, the work and the psyches of Ann Taylor and Georgia O'Keeffe. O'Keeffe spent her early years as an artist in New York, with occasional visits to Lake George in the Adirondacks. She made many excursions to the Southwest, and finally succumbed to its magnetism. What they have in common in their work is perhaps only the exploration of natural phenomena as a basic subject. The major similarity is apparent in the solitude necessary to their lives and the singlemindedness of their artistic intentions: "It is not so much her work that I admire, although she has made some wonderful paintings, but Georgia O'Keeffe as a person—intelligent, passionate, disciplined, sensitive and wholly immersed in her art."

What Ann Taylor learned from nature, what any artist learns from nature, is simply to stand back and select, to absorb the essence of a scene. Selection, certainly, is at the core of Georgia O'Keeffe's flat, patterned concepts. Taylor, too, chooses patterns out of natural form, but the resemblance to the actual reference is maintained. With O'Keeffe, the latitude between clear recognition and abstraction is so extreme that the image fades to areas of wash—pigment as pigment—although the gray hills of New Mexico with their furrows and ridges remain tied to that region.

For Taylor, the drive is to express the essence, not the particulars, of experienced scenes. The aim is also expressed by O'Keeffe in her autobiography, **Georgia O'Keeffe** (Viking): "I long ago came to the conclusion that even if I could put down accurately the thing that I saw and enjoyed, it would not give the observer the kind of feeling it gave me. I had to create an equivalent for what I felt about what I was looking at, not copy it." This is the essential element, the inferred source of universalities, that both Taylor and O'Keeffe extract from landscape.

By early 1980, established in her own studio in Scottsdale, Ann again began to paint in oil. She found that her study of lithography and watercolor was a stimulus for a new series as she returned to her familiar, original medium. **Leveling,** a transplant of the shadowy, mysterious mesa silhouettes which dominated her work of previous years, contains no wisps of fog or mists but has a rather streaked sky, not moisture-laden, but dry and brilliant like the West's. The streaked pattern was an inheritance from the transfer of media, the trip from watercolor into oil. The bleeding properties of the thin, transparent medium are intentionally emphasized. It is characteristic of Ann's use of oil that, however thickly she applies the pigment, and often it is very thickly applied, the outcome appears thin because of the extreme smoothness of the surface.

Leveling 1979
46" by 46"
oil on canvas

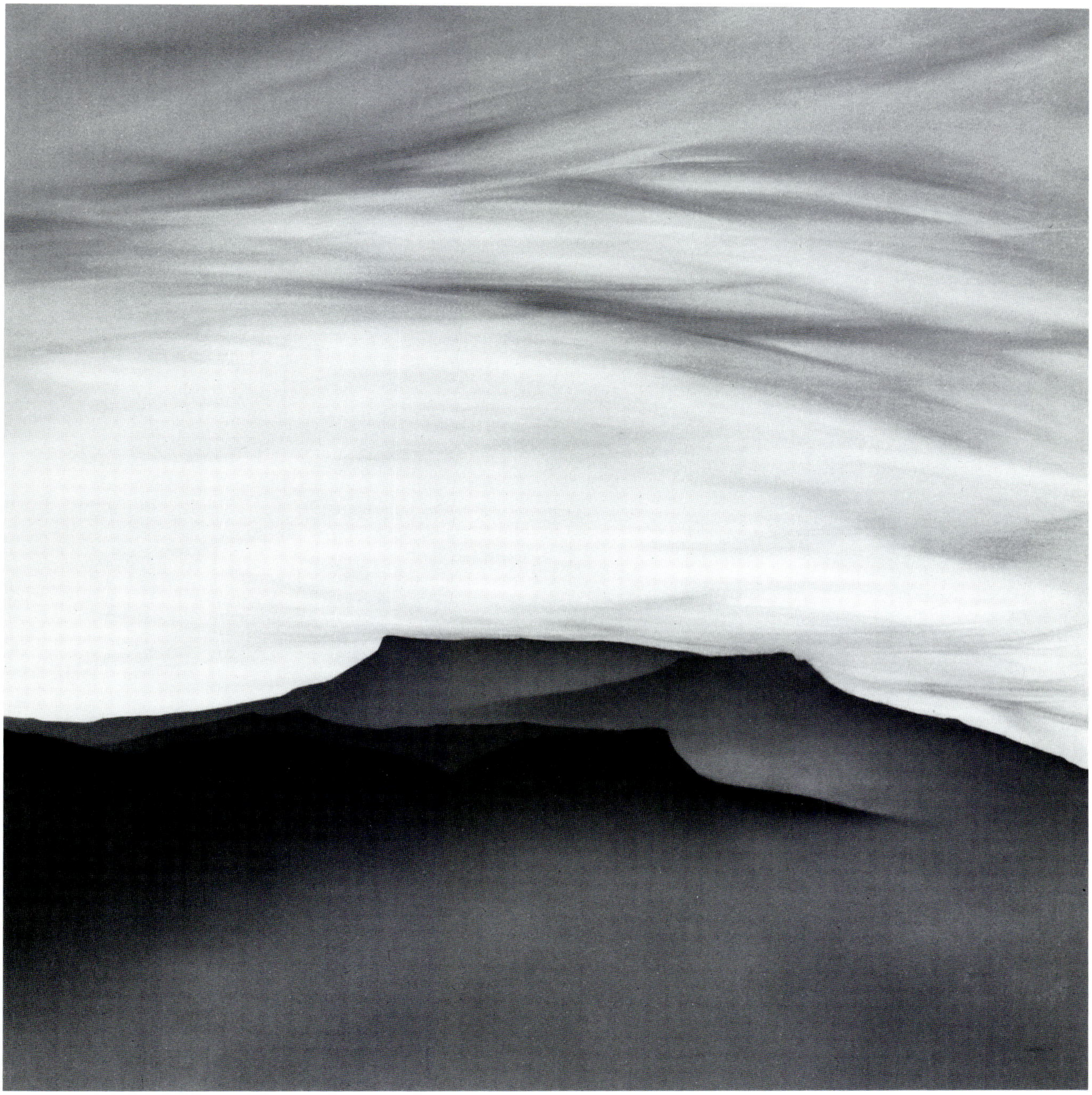

Blue Living 1980
46″ by 46″
oil on canvas

In **Blue Living,** these streaks and overlays are combined in the lower portion of the painting to represent land: "I am reminded of some of the beautiful country to the north on the Navajo Reservation. There you can see a crisscross of roads that looks like a linear pattern laid on top of the varying colors and forms of the land. It is lovely—very understated. There is a direct relationship between the sky in **Leveling** and the land in **Blue Living.** The sky evolved out of the transfer from watercolor techniques, and then the land-form developed out of that. It's a direct link of pictorial ideas. Whenever I come up with a new idea, I use it alone on a few canvases and then in conjunction with other ideas from previous paintings."

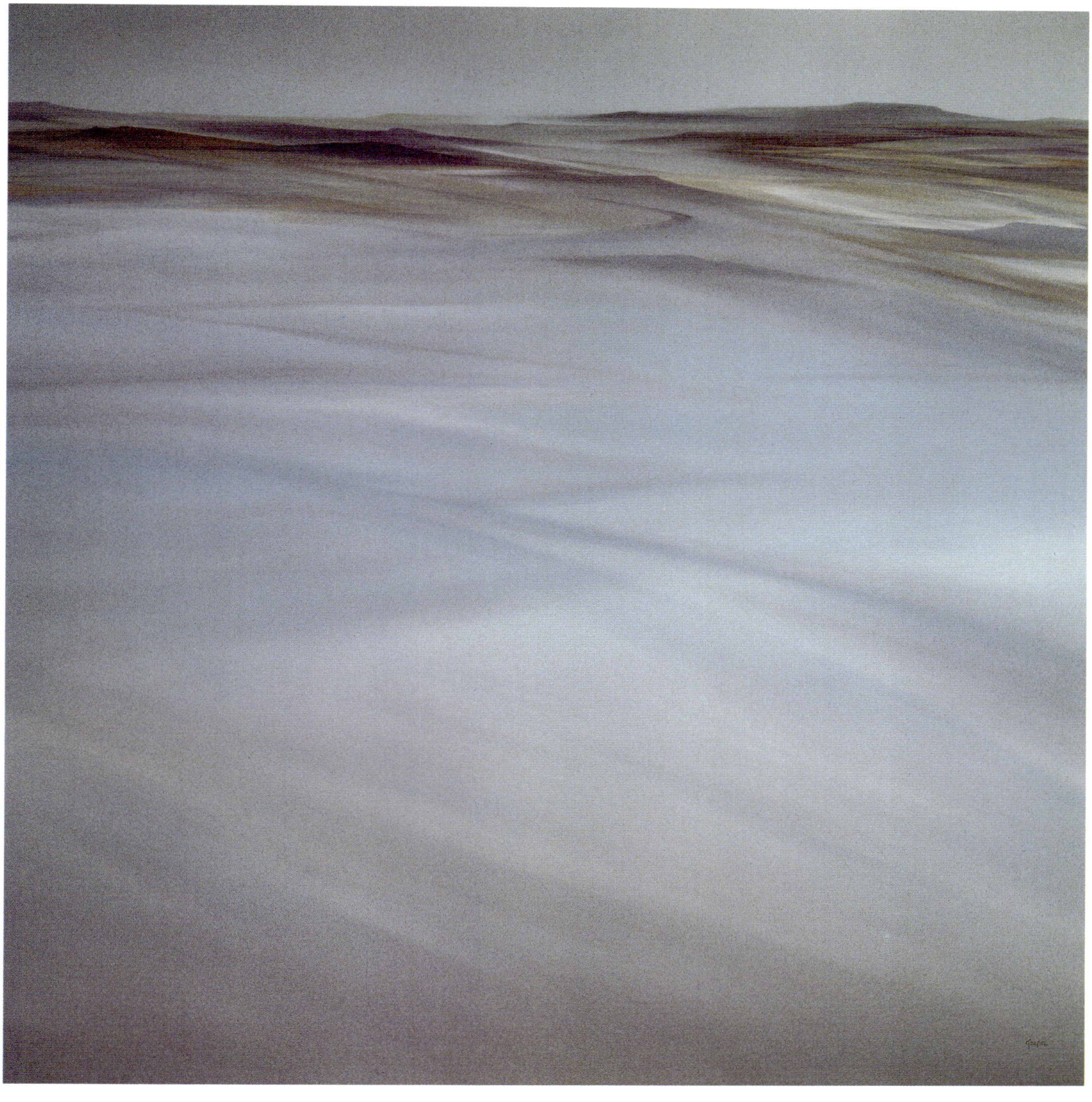

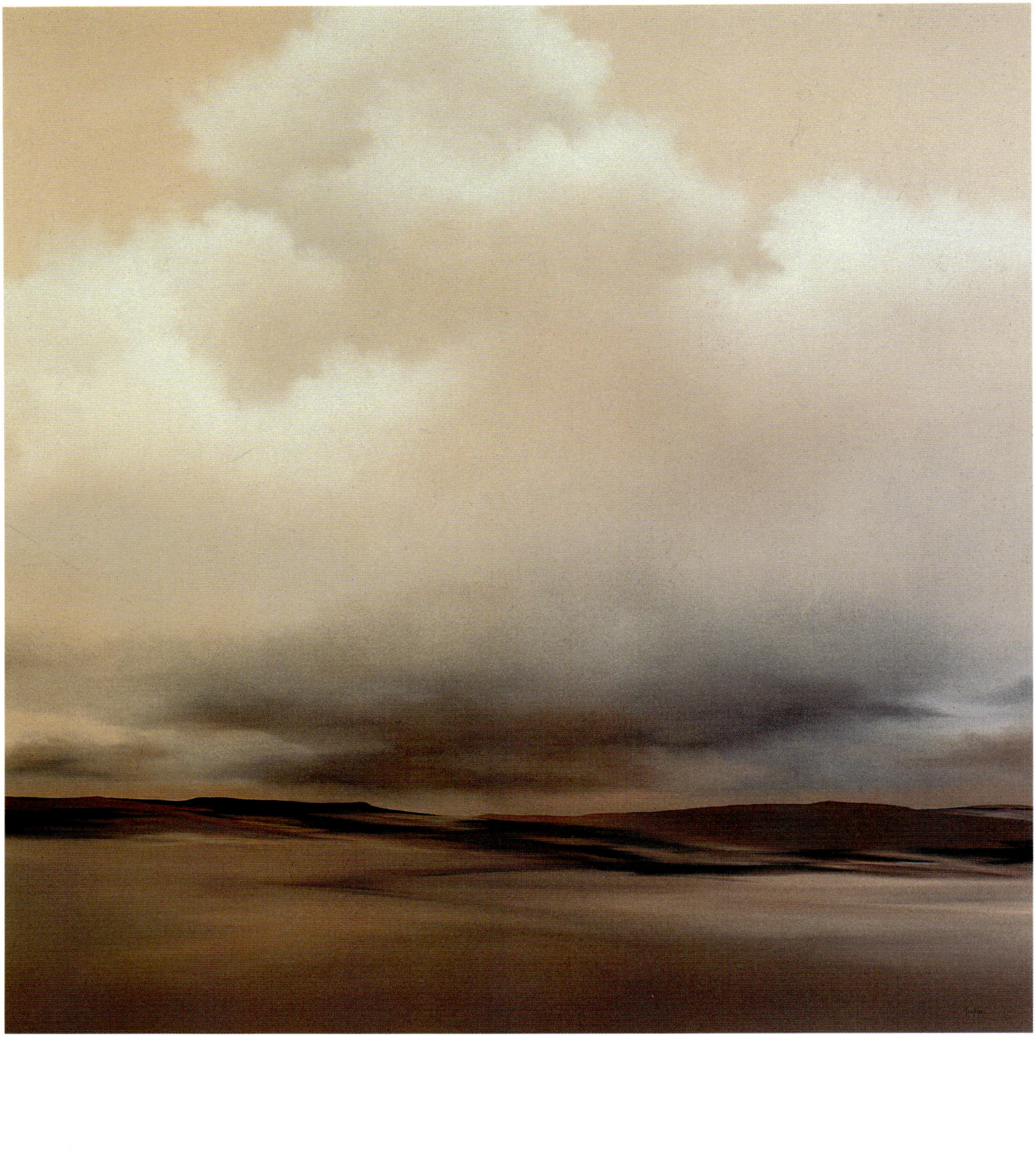

Celebration is another component in this serial chain. It is a synthesis of the mature rendering of clouds and the cross-hatched linear roads of **Blue Living.** Here the flowing lines have come to earth, creating a tender, bosoming spread of hills—the soft, warm brown of the western landscape unalloyed by noticeable growth. Towering cloud-formations, edged in white, deepen into the steel gray of threatening storm clouds. They hover above the shallow zigzag of distant uplands, visible more clearly in the West where the eye can reach, unimpeded, for miles. **Celebration** brings together ideas from several painting phases and holds them in equilibrium.

Celebration 1980
46″ by 46″
oil on canvas

Even as the number of her collectors grew, Ann continued to keep track of each painting and its location. She shared the publicity and reviews pertaining to each exhibition with all who owned examples of her work, thus also informing them of her developing artistic ideas. Her friend and collector, Racey Gilbert, responded to seeing this fresh series of paintings: "I am amazed by your growth and openness. I see how the place captures your fancy and I recognize the openness that is you as I feel you drinking in new concepts. The definition of the ground is forming, the colors of the sky are changed, there is more geometry and less of the murky fuzzy vapors; the light is abstracted into more solid shapes; knives of color, wedges of ground, and colors, new colors; a new palette evolves as the place of being becomes absorbed in the becoming. Oh, levels of representation; oh, masks in the dance!"

The developments and transitions that were happening in these paintings seem, in retrospect, to parallel the impact that Ann's move to the West had on her life. It had taken a certain courage to leave the safe, controlled world of the East where life was predictable, neatly in balance, and try out new footing in the West. However unsettling at first, the freedom gained opened up new vistas both geographic and artistic. The far horizons of the West were real and exciting. In that immensely diverse topography, Ann made long solo drives into stretches of unsettled country, deep into the reservation lands where it was very beautiful but harsh: "Although I am comfortable in a sophisticated urban environment, when I am behind the wheel I can let my mind wander and go free. There has to be a touching with the land. It is another facet of myself. It keeps me whole."

A hint of an emerging interest in being out on the road appears first in the aptly titled painting **Transition.** In the foreground, zigzag shapes recede toward the distant range. This is a pictorial device that directs the eye, but it is also evidence of a new concern with linear composition. Illumination is felt, not focused in a single source. It is wider and more diffused than, say, the localized light of **Afternoon Pond.** Details are not defined. There is instead a reach for distant views—the mood of the whole. Interestingly, the clouds have also changed, taking on a wispy look unrelated to the cumulus mounds which, in earlier work, piled themselves above land and water. These clouds demonstrate further incorporation of her watercolor techniques.

Transition 1979
40″ by 50″
oil on canvas

During the following year the tranquil, veiled landscapes gave way to a more dynamic vision. More and more strongly, Ann was moved to paint the sensation of motion, of velocity, of moving in or out of the landscape—to simulate on the two-dimensional plane of the canvas the sensation of speed, which in itself has no conventional dimensions.

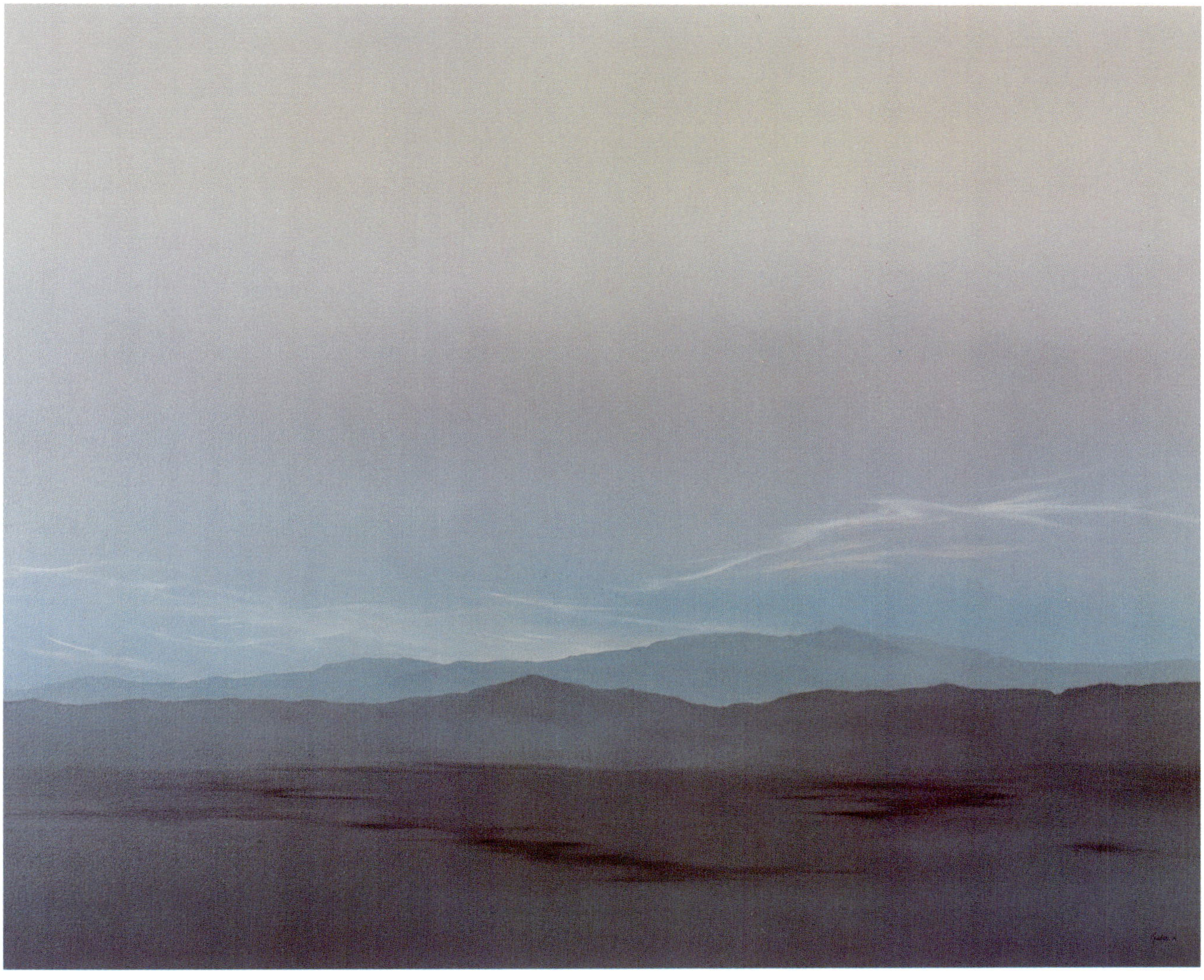

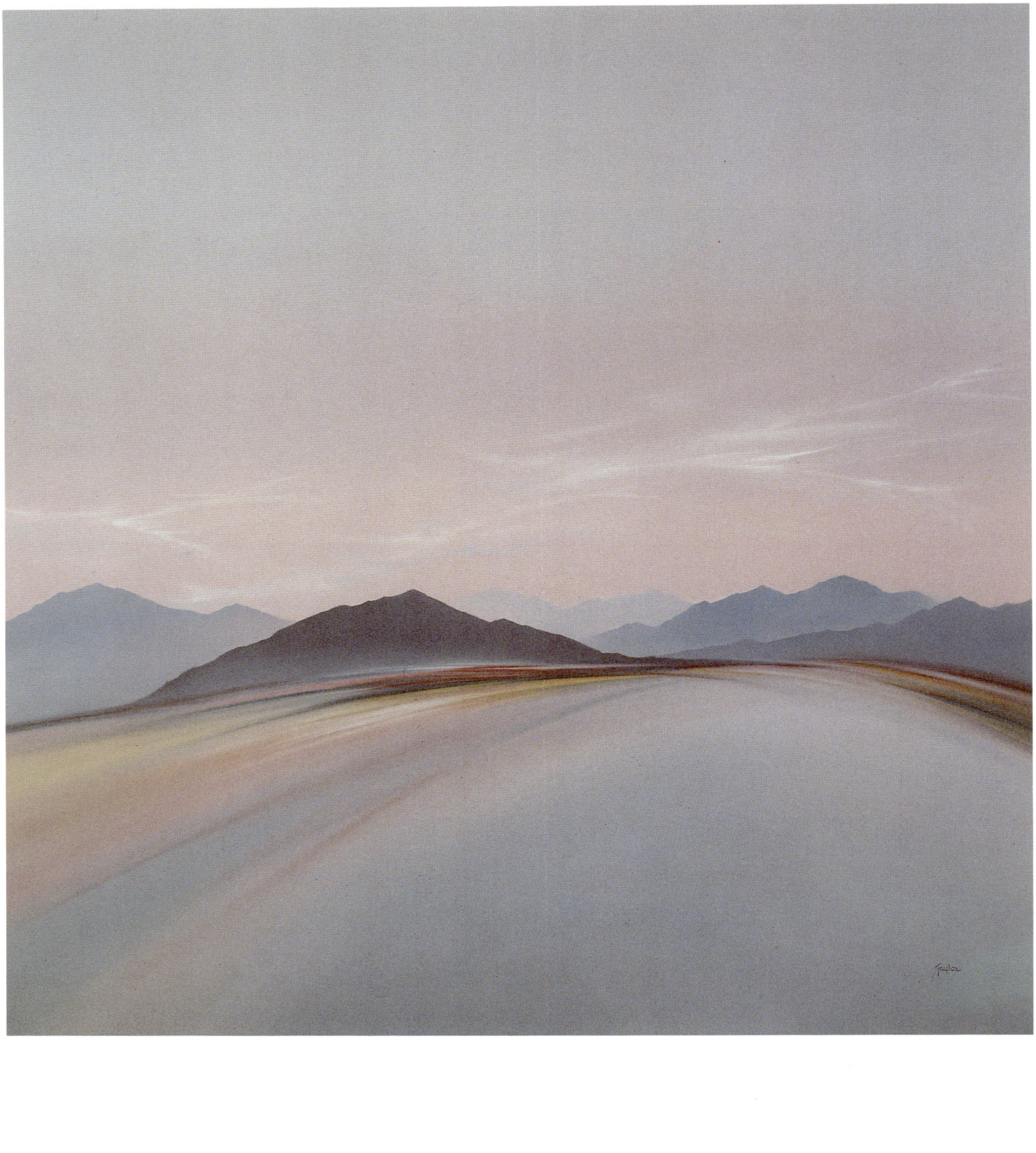

Lavender West is a work which bridges the ideas expressed in **Transition** and those of the later, more abstracted **Acceleration** paintings. It is recognizably a landscape derived from western experience. As in **Transition,** the atmosphere appears clear with no clouds except for a few threadlike traces which gently recapitulate the nervous, angular contours of the mountains and mirror the long ribbons of color in the foreground. The mountain shapes, flat and reduced to simple outlines, break the two areas, sky and earth, and act as a baffle between the tranquility of the sky and movement in the foreground. Force is projected against its opposite.

Life for Ann, once more centered on her art. Her thinking had been stretched, extending the boundaries of her life and her painting. It was important to find the right house for herself and her daughter and a working space for painting. She purchased a townhouse in Scottsdale—a modern two-bedroom condominium, the design of which pivoted around an open, two-story living room. Its spacious white walls became filled with paintings, the courtyards, front and back, with sculpture: "I began collecting art and displaying it alongside my own work. The execution of ideas by other artists is of great interest to me, particularly in sculpture. Both the tactile and the visual surfaces of three-dimensional work are wonderfully exciting."

Lavender West 1980
40" by 40"
oil on canvas

Ann's surroundings, fitting them to herself and her work, have always been important. From the days when she first decorated her dormitory room at Vassar by clearing it out and putting her few furnishings on the floor, beautiful and consistent living space had been a necessity. As an artist friend, Genevieve Reckling, once remarked: "It's amazing. Everything in your whole life relates to everything else, from your paintings to the way you arrange your furniture, right down to your knives and forks." This house in Arizona contained a minimum of furniture, each piece having been carefully chosen for its elegance of design, and a maximum of art—painting, sculpture, photographs, ceramics.

At first Ann converted her garage into a studio. Later she rented a working space several miles away: "Painting involves intense concentration and total commitment. There were too many distractions for me, working at home. In New York and in Garrison, my studio space was a walking distance from where I lived. That separation is essential. While I am working, my mind is totally absorbed in the painting. When I leave the studio, sometimes as soon as the door is closed, the painting is completely in another place in my head and often I do not even have the memory of it. But as soon as I come back to the studio for the next session and my hand is on the door, I am totally involved again."

Ann's painting continued to express a distortion of the land, as though a metaphor of speed could be captured on the static canvas. A specific incident occurred: "I flew East and on the plane happened to see a magazine article about hang gliding. The photographs were fascinating because the landscape in the background was on a tilt. When I returned to the paintings, I decided to turn the horizon to a nearly forty-five degree angle. Suddenly one had the sense of speed as one would feel it either on the ground or in the air."

Current Madness 1981
50″ by 48″
oil on canvas

The result was **Current Madness,** a key painting in the **Acceleration Series,** and a turning point in her artistic concerns. The basic intent is very different from any earlier work. It is a dynamic sweep of motion as opposed to a quiet contemplation. The road leads in and out of the field of vision, providing both an external and an internal sensation. Lines of force converge at a point nearly outside of the painting's frame. A dramatic tilt shifts the horizon, denying the solid flatness of the earth, its weight and stillness. The viewer is left off balance, adrift in a vortex dizzying the senses. The composition reiterates the conceptual quality of physical sensation; the vast stretch of foreground is offset by the rhythmical layering of the diagonal ridges.

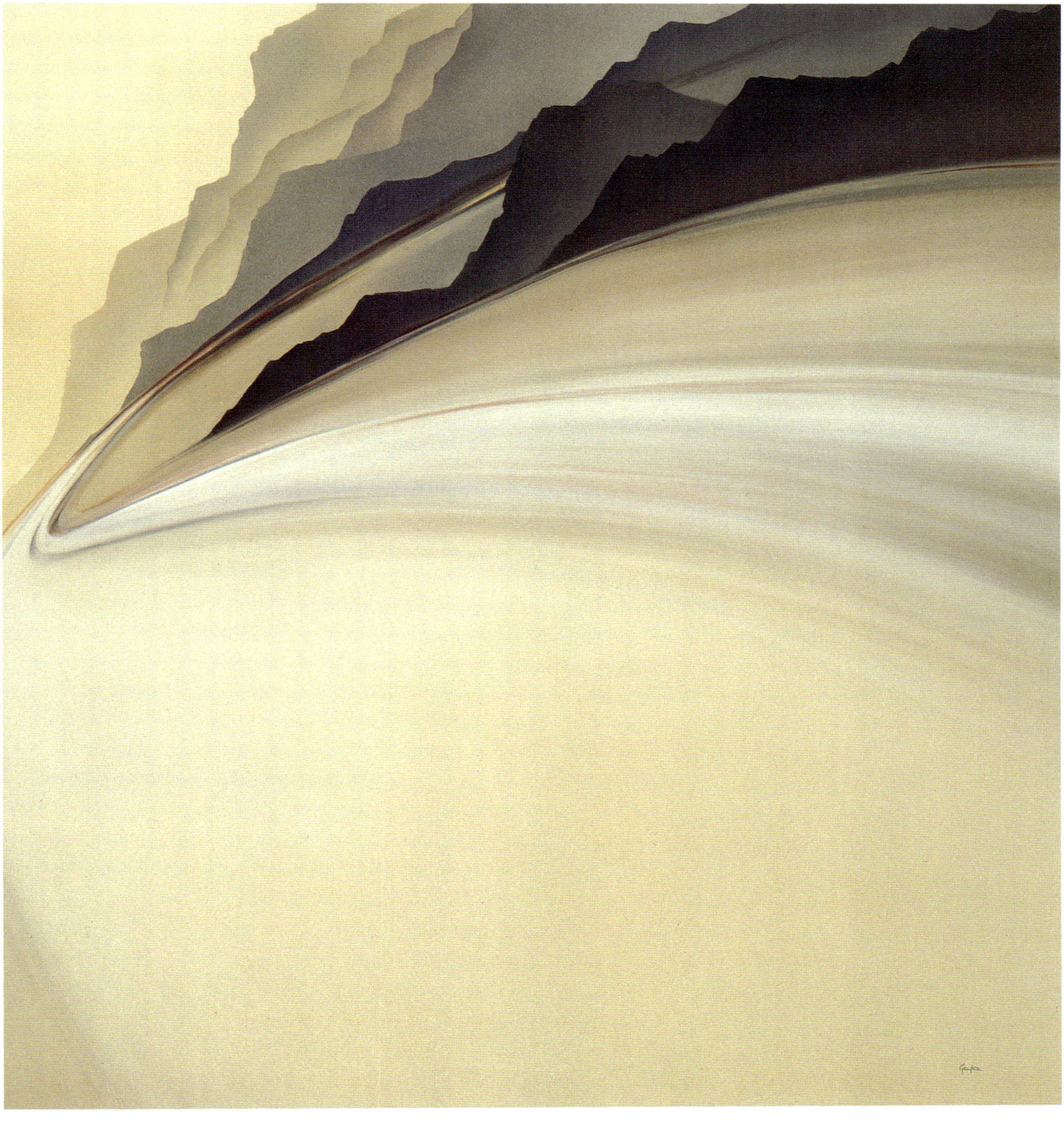

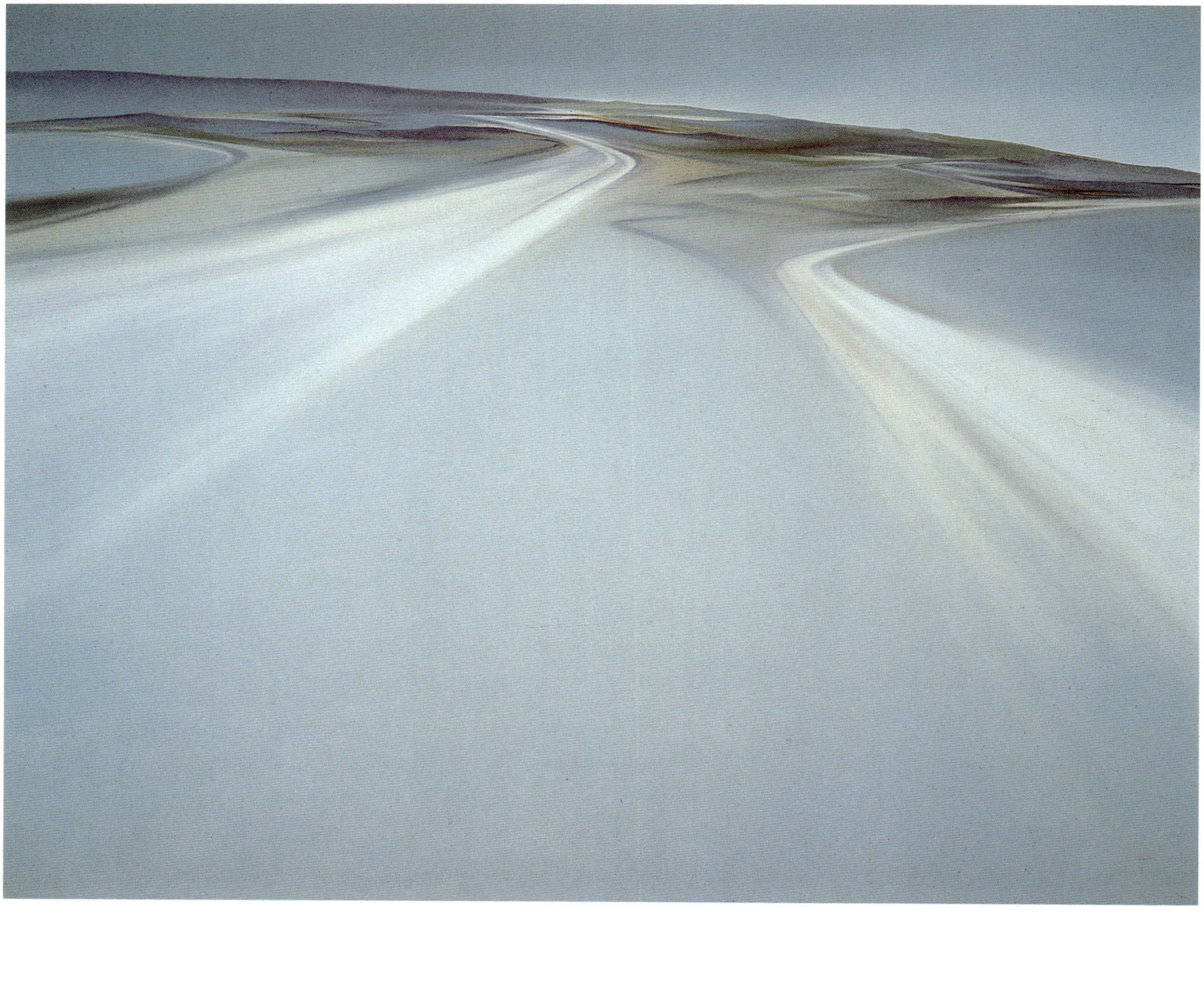

As any particular series progresses, the work often becomes visibly more abstract. **Rotation** is an extension of the earlier **Acceleration** paintings. The base in nature has nearly melted into pure abstraction, the land forms are barely recognizable. It does more than depict speed; it comes close to the jumping off place. Its subtleties depend on the finest gradations made possible by the glass-smooth surface of the oil which allows no shadow of a brushstroke, no hint of texture to disturb it. In this space, blue, like the atmosphere, takes over the role of definition. There is the merest sketch of undulation at the horizon's edge. The real subject is a concept: the curvature of the earth: "Speed bends and blurs the contours of reality. It is challenging and exciting to evoke feelings in the observer that are sensory as well as intellectual and emotional."

The ferocity and fragility of the desert environment, and the clarity of the light in Arizona affected Ann's palette. Her paintings were no longer simply gradations of muted color. They were intensified—a saturation of opalescent hues.

Rotation 1981
46″ by 62″
oil on canvas

Richard Diebenkorn, who worked in a strongly abstract mode during the time he painted in New Mexico, sensed similar colors in the desert's light and space. He reacted with pinks and yellows and other high-keyed tones in his Albuquerque paintings. He saw the orchestration of these bright hues as a working principle, "forming with color." Diebenkorn's inspiration came from the land, expressed intuitively, figurative or not. As with Ann Taylor's work, the landscape is seen as the artist's initial impetus, the wellspring of contemplation.

Diebenkorn, though, through his splashy brushwork, betrayed an almost chaotic energy beneath the highly colored surface. He allowed, even exploited, change and impulse in the course of each painting. All this is foreign to the smooth serenity of Taylor's surfaces, calculated to reflect a state of mind, not the process of making: "It is not to demonstrate my hand on the canvas that is important, but rather to reveal my head. And my feeling."

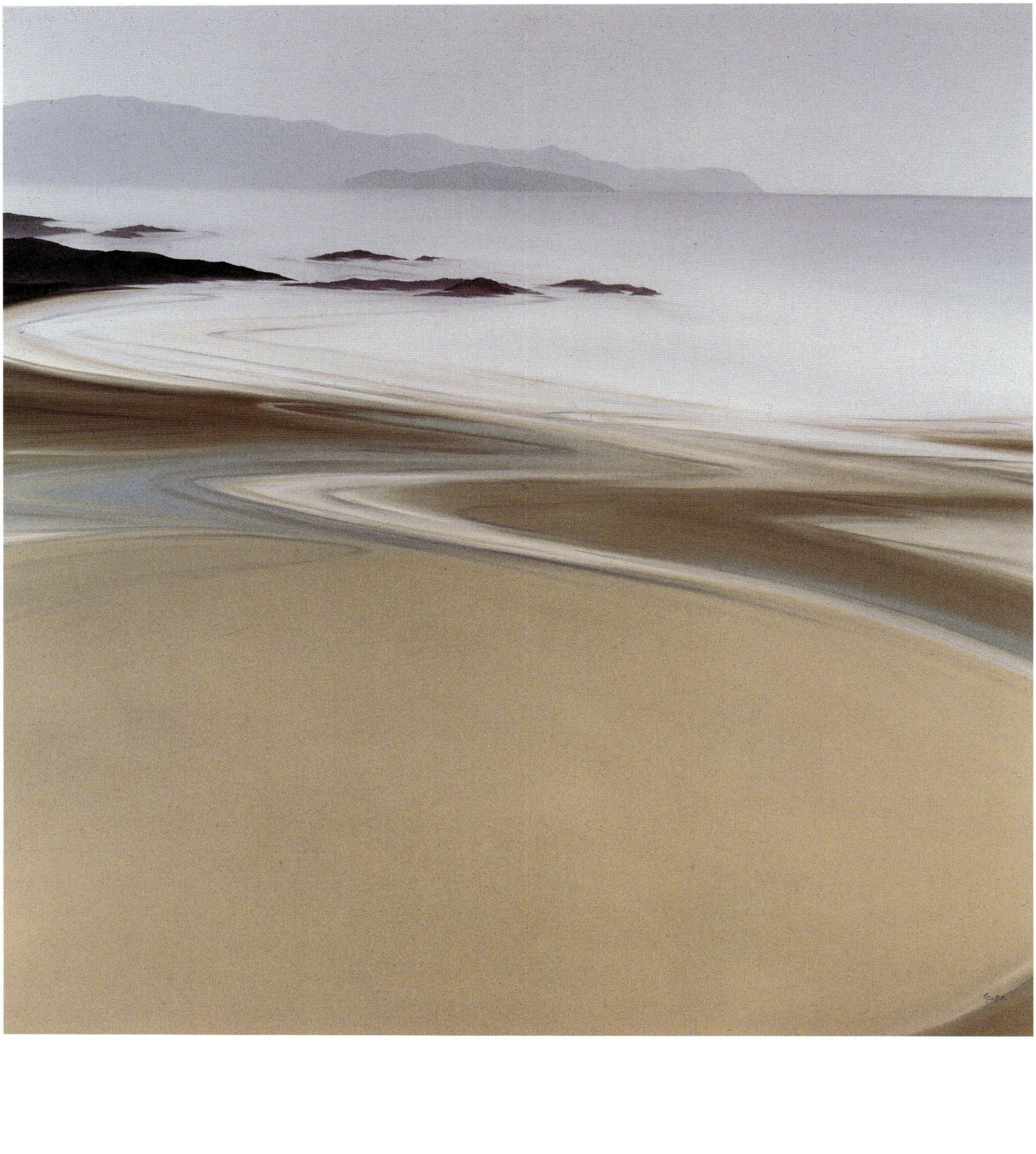

Prestwick Departure 1981
44″ by 44″
oil on canvas

Concurrent with this expansion of color and sensation in her painting, Ann found new freedom of action. Familiar as she was with the landscape of America, she was also curious about variations in terrain which might increase her visual awareness. In the summer of 1981, she contacted a group of her collectors who agreed to sponsor a summer abroad in Europe and the British Isles in exchange for paintings to be executed upon her return. For nine weeks Ann traveled in Europe, first visiting the great museums of Paris and London and then driving around the countryside of the British Isles. She found the Old World landscape as lovely as expected, but not as different as she had anticipated.

Strikingly, however, the pictorial themes of the **Acceleration Series,** familiar and tested, fit in this different context. The patterns, extracted from nature and converted by the mind of the artist, again conformed to a multitude of subjects. **Prestwick Departure** is an example. Its subject, a tidal estuary, differs from those of the American landscape, but the motifs of unimpeded sweep to the horizon line—a curve of speed leaping out from the patterns of tidemarks and the sea—read as the theme of acceleration in new guise. Color, however, perhaps influenced by the overcast Scottish skies, has made a return to the natural. It is as if, beneath the surface, color had been laid over an independent base of form.

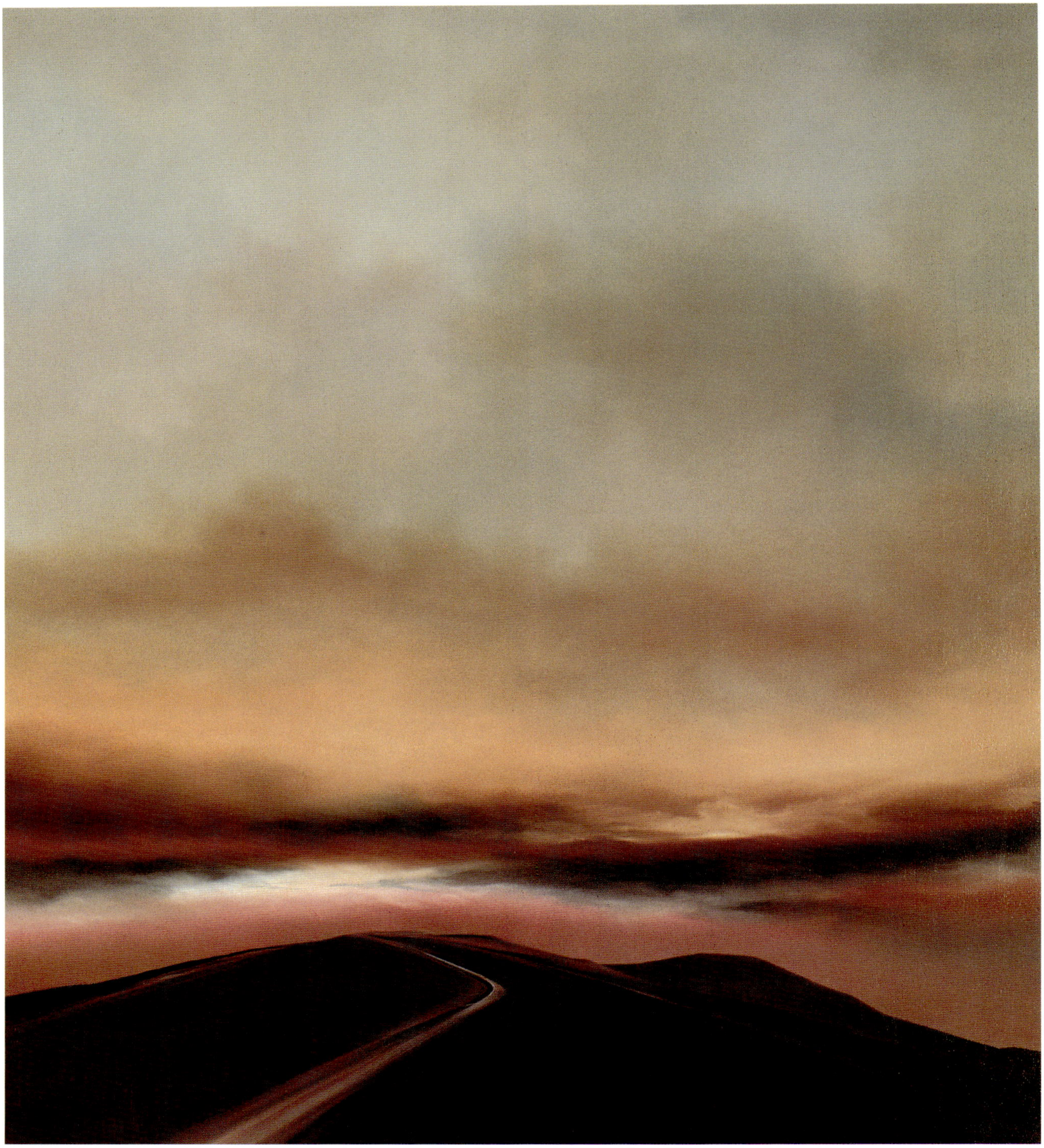

Anticipated Heather 1981
46″ by 42″
oil on canvas

Also from the sponsored summer abroad, **Anticipated Heather** brings together threads from other works—cloud, land and motion. Light striking through the clouds, at their deepest and most intense near the horizon, creates a focus. The configuration of the dark clouds, the underside of fleecy beds of vapor, mirrors the shallow, inverted "V" of the dark ground. Here, as in the early Lake Placid paintings, a rhythm of repeated forms occurs. But the distinctive difference, again, is one of mood: a feeling of something impending. Perhaps it is only a weather change, but the impression is distinctly romantic, a matter of emotion. Even in these invariably empty vistas, where people never appear, the important person, the viewing intelligence, is the filter through which the impression is received. This image is, then, unimpeachably subjective, albeit void of particular features.

Red Riding stands as a nearly monumental work, synthesizing the major themes of a decade of Taylor paintings. Clouds play a role in it and so does the ground with its sweep of onrushing road. The distant horizon slants, intensifying the notion of acceleration that informs the work.

On first viewing, this painting seems to be related to John Constable's great views of clouds and sunsets over Hampstead Heath. As in **Red Riding,** a Constable sky appears incandescent. The source of light seems not to be in the sky but *is* the sky. Lofty clouds are piled heavenward, and out of them a luminosity infuses the painting.

But beyond the surface similarity, the approaches of these two artists are categorically divergent. Constable loved and sought out the "particular" of any scene. He looked keenly at the sky, observing its every color change and cloud formation. To him, each particular of cloud and sun and wind was remarkable, as characteristic as Salisbury's spires. He painted to portray verisimilitude; though, great as he was, it was verisimilitude of the spirit, not the letter, which he achieved.

Ann Taylor seeks to reveal the "universal" rather than the "particular"—an essential difference from Constable. From a given distance, her paintings seem, to a greater or lesser degree, real. Closer inspection reveals that they are built from tiny symbols, a cryptic shorthand based on interlace, on delicately feathered edges, on scallops, hatches, enamel-like sheets of glaze. The color is not an imitation of nature, despite coincidental similarity, but is a matter of the artist's choice.

It is possible, then, to go on into **Red Riding** and suspend belief, to enter it as an evocation of landscape remembered, as in a dream, the details lost or shading into obscurity. This painting is not a record of the day, the hour, the wind velocity. It is essence distilled. Yet, by going still deeper, it is possible to discern a bond between the naturalistic and the idealizing view. The appreciation, the contemplation, the wish to recreate feeling as well as appearance is romantic, and the romantic attitude, realistically or abstractly expressed, is the real basis of the work. **Red Riding,** whatever its source, comes together as a celebration of living.

Red Riding 1982
90" by 52"
oil on canvas

Those far reaches which we traverse only in our minds, whose visible outline comes through only faintly, like a ghost image on an ancient vellum, gain clear expression in the Ann Taylor landscape. That far reach, the "other side" so to speak, is the search for universality that Ann Taylor is working to express.

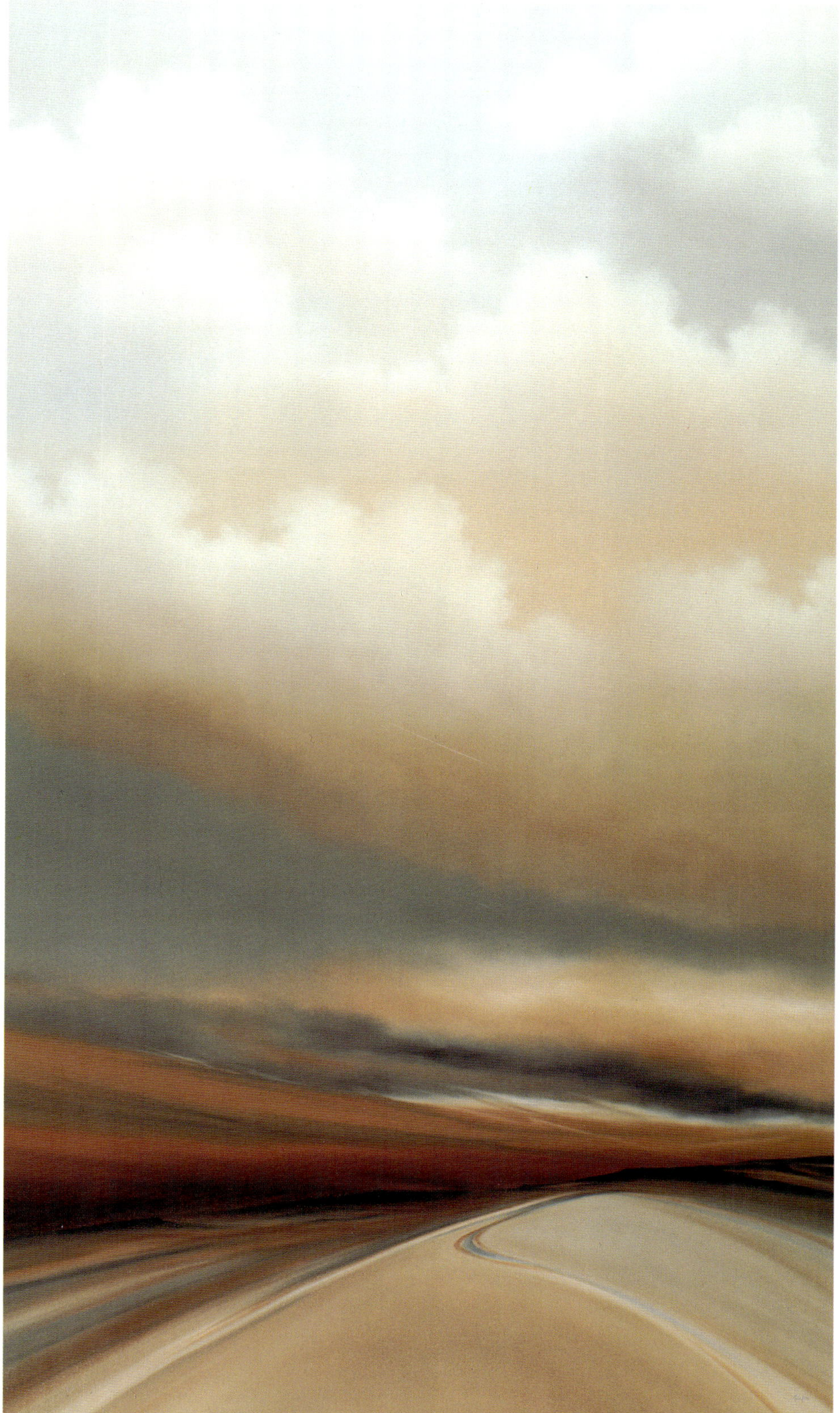

Chapter Four: The Reach of Solitude

"One of my desires is to make purely abstract art; art which does not refer to realistic form, but rather art whose source is solely my own aesthetic sense. Nothing more."

Technical capacity was finally and surely in Ann's possession now—that elusive mastery of materials which allows the artist to assume the means and focus on the spirit. She could rely on her ability to create a smooth, clear, even surface. The interaction between the right ground over the right canvas and the right consistency of pigment could be taken for granted. At this stage in an artist's life, intellectual questions—the requirements not of hand and eye but of the governing mind—become the intense immediate concern.

More than ever Ann felt the need to analyze, to try to define what she had done and what she hoped to do. As she conceived it, hers was an art of the "interior self," but what, at base, was that? How did such an art differ from, say, the directly recorded impression, as in Monet? From the completely abstracted, as in Mondrian? What are its related forms of expression, what its opposites?

An art of the interior self begins in contemplation. To contemplate in turn requires experience to commence and to sustain it, and this experience, to reach the inner self, must pass through the vehicle of perception. Clearly then, the first roots of such an art are to be found in perception. Through perception the exterior world is experienced and becomes the interior self—that self which lies beyond the known boundaries of things: the reach of solitude. Through contemplation and the analysis of recorded impression, the image is transmuted into idealized type.

To exemplify the ideal the artist must reach for essentials and disregard accidents of time and place so that the transient world becomes the universe within the mind. Ann realized that the elimination of the circumstances of particular experience was the first step, the consistent unifying link, in all her work. For her, first the experience and then the departing from it—crossing the boundary of the particular and reaching for the transcendental—was the goal. A friend, Sophia Klonick, responding to her painting wrote: "There certainly can be no great art without some philosophy behind it, without someone who has thought profoundly of life and nature. The true artist, like the philosopher, is a searcher after truth: not cold, objective truth, but truth which is its own testimony and which is carried alive in the heart by passion."

An artist who understood this truth and whose paintings come together as moments of contemplation committed as paint was Mark Rothko. For him, as for Ann Taylor, the source of the work was landscape. It is important, though, that it was not the experience of landscape condensed, but the contemplation of that experience, that fed his creative springs. A long meditation over nature, the movements of the clouds, the diffraction of light, were interpreted by Rothko and transmitted to the canvas. It was the artist's expectation that it would be so translated that the observer too might reflect on the light and color in which, on this many-colored earth, we live. It was the essence of the dream, not the outlines, he willed through paint and canvas, to convey. Describing his methods, he wrote: "Neither the action nor the actors can be anticipated, or described in advance. They begin as an adventure in an unknown space. It is at the moment of completion that in a flash of recognition they are seen to have the quality and function that was intended. Ideas and plans which existed in the mind at the start were simply the doorway through which one left the world in which they occur."

With this kind of thinking Ann Taylor feels a strong affinity. "Ideas and plans" for any given painting exist in her mind as the work begins. Nevertheless, in the process of painting, strong intuitive decisions sustain its momentum. Only upon completion is the work revealed in its entirety to her intellectual consciousness.

"Honing down to essential elements is my primary concern. It is a classical principle. It also links to oriental philosophies. My work does not emphasize the replication of actual experience. It deals with ideas, with finding and portraying these ideas on canvas." People often stop the artist to say they have witnessed an "Ann Taylor sky" or an "Ann Taylor mountain range." Her paintings have struck a chord that is spiritual and thus universal. This occurrence precipitates a paradox; the viewers see nature as imitating art. What has really happened is that they have witnessed some particular version of the idealized type of landscape which she paints. They have fitted their personal experience to the painted prototype. Nature in the wild—profuse, detailed, asymmetrical, undisciplined—has been made to conform to the mental grid provided by the artist. These paintings are distillations of the essential elements of landscape, nature as the mind reorders it.

Although she looks ahead to the possibility of completely abstract art, Ann Taylor is currently producing work that contains a fullness, a richness of image abstracted from but not separate from the natural world. The leap into pure abstraction has not yet been made, her footing is still on the firm ground above the precipice. She is well aware, though, that even for Piet Mondrian, that great proponent of the toally abstract, experience began with natural things as familiar and homely as houses, chrysanthemums and seascapes. He, too, found that the path to the universal lies in the "honing down" to essentials. Although his final paintings depict nothing more than pure color, space and line, as spare and severe as it is possible to get, he began with representation. In summing up the search for ultimate expression, he said: "Even though we never find unity expressed exactly, we can unify every representation. In other words, the exact representation of unity can be expressed, it must be expressed, for it is not visible in concrete reality." In seeking the universal, he rejected the particular. To this dictum, Taylor willingly subscribes.

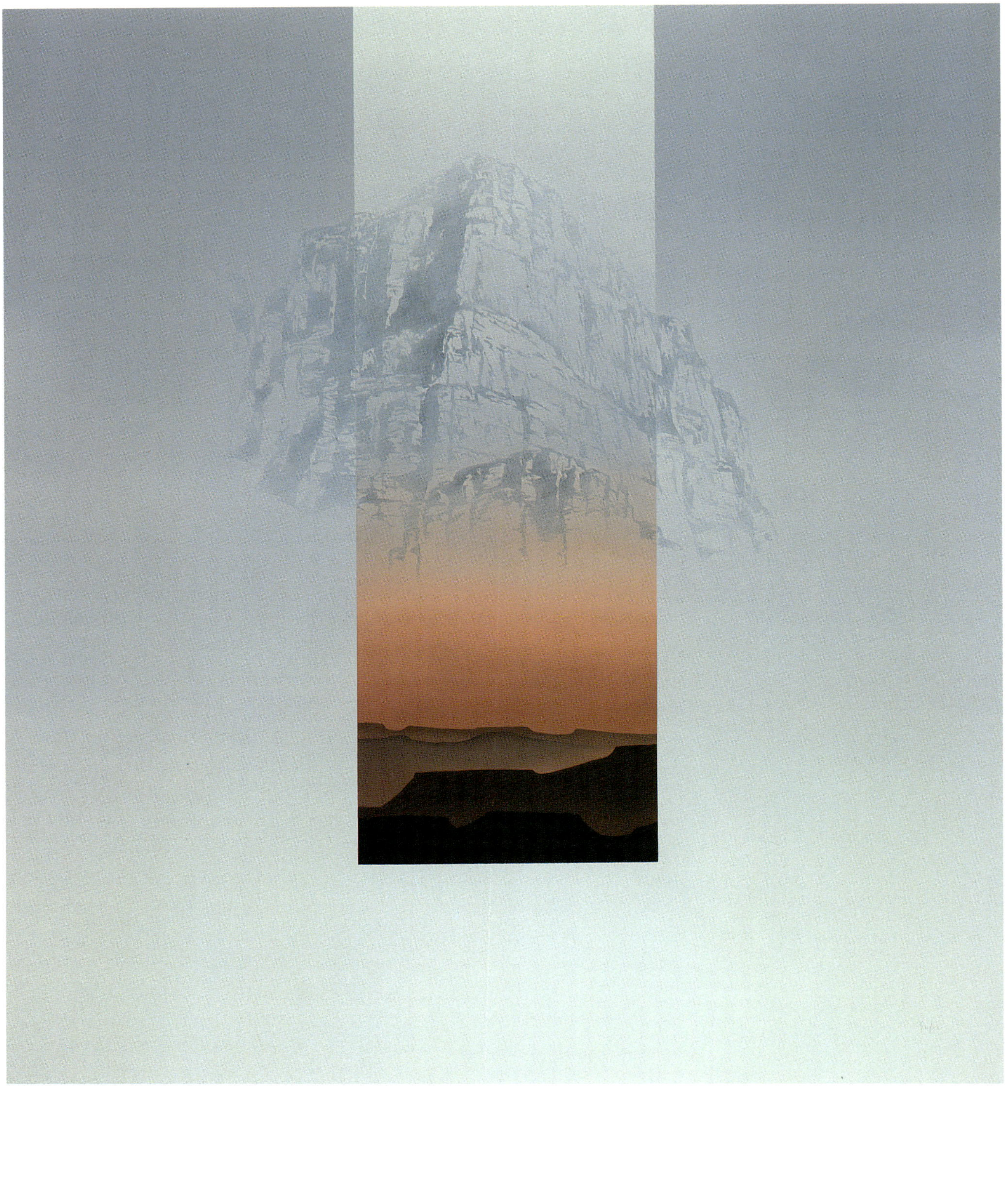

Canyon Ghost 1982
52″ by 48″
oil on canvas

Ann Taylor's recent work concentrates entirely on the search for the universal and constitutes a dramatic swing toward the abstract. In the series **Windows, Rearview Mirrors and Ghosts,** multiple pictorial elements have been introduced. The canvases are divided into geometric areas of pure color into which one or more schematized landscape motif is set in contrast. In **Canyon Ghost** for instance, two landscape images are superimposed over an abstract field of graded color. The "ghost" image, a pale detail of canyon walls, delicately drawn, floats above the more generalized aerial view of the canyon whole. This duality creates a painting charged with energy. The work is half the natural sky with its layers of color, blue which deepens with the distance, and half an abstract space division, like the architecture of a dream. This division evokes a wall—a seamless wall, having no mortar and no chinks, no trace of workmen's hands: it is a creature of the mind, solely. It is as though the subject, in this case the Grand Canyon, was being examined for both its cosmic and its physical impact.

The series deals with a complex balance between forms that have reference to landscape and those that are totally non-objective: "I continue to create paintings that exist on levels of both external and internal reality. The viewer is immediately excited by the familiar, the recognizable. The deeper, more contemplative qualities appear gradually. The new series tries to suspend these levels in counterpoint. I remember while driving through the countryside being aware that I could focus on one image through the windshield and a different image in the rearview mirror at the same time. It occurred to me that a viewer could assimilate two or more images simultaneously on a canvas. It also gave me a vehicle for incorporating into one painting not only an abstract element versus a realistic one, but also detail versus 'the grand view.' "

If the mind is itself a window, not dependent on the physical properties of glass, the painting, **Window with Pink Shimmer,** for example, gives the metaphor a simple, striking shape. Through it we see the Taylor image of the world, pure and ideal. The classical view has always stressed plastic values: the clear line, the palpable form, as opposed to "painterly, coloristic romanticism." It is Poussin versus Delacroix, Cézanne at the opposite end of the table from Van Gogh. In contrast, Taylor's meditative evocations of the inward view are defined, intransigently there. Most recently, as in **Canyon Ghost** and **Window with Pink Shimmer,** her work has taken on more and more concrete contours, almost as precise as engineering renderings, except that the bridges she renders stretch from the outward to the inner world and then back out. These paintings are thus a picture of the picturing of the world. They represent the way all of us, in varying degrees, view the world through the filter of ourselves.

Window with Pink Shimmer 1982
42″ by 46″
oil on canvas

Ann Taylor has been painting steadily since 1961. In reviewing her first exhibition in New York, Jane Jaffe Young wrote: "There is an aura of spirituality in these paintings that stems from the austere simplicity of design, the subtlety of color, and, most of all, from the underlying intensity and single-mindedness of the artist's vision." Remarkably, this vision has found full expression in her most recent work.

Hers is western meditation, the synthesizing, pantheistic attitude that has its roots in Concord, not Kyoto. So, the mountain that has always been a visible manifestation of the upward striving from within becomes, in a Taylor painting, an idealized figure for man's view of nature. It is regularized, stripped of the accident of circumstance, but still, recognizably, the world he inhabits and sees. The sky, seeming perhaps as real in her painting as in the image in a photograph, is still her idealized version of the sky, not that recorded on the retina but that created from the mind.

What the observer has, then, in a larger view of the Taylor painting, is the record of the artist observing the world, the bright pageant as it passes across the inner range of her mind. Just as we cannot visualize without the model from physics which even the metaphor, "the inner mind," suggests, so the paintings of Ann Taylor must be written in a language expressing the symbols of things, their counterparts, not their selves.

In her quest to reach inside herself, to challenge and discover the consummate potential of her resources, Ann Taylor has created a body of paintings, nearing seven hundred in number. From the insular experience of her personal life, she has brought forth images which cause the viewer to contemplate on dimensions in his own spirit. They acknowledge the beauty which lies in the mysterious unknown and the value of contemplation. This is meditation made visible—the reach of solitude.

Biographical Outline

1941 Born on March 23 in Rochester, New York, the first of four children of Joseph William Taylor and Helen Atkins Taggart.

1946–1958 Attended Allen Creek School, a public elementary school through the eighth grade and Columbia School, a college preparatory school for girls, from which she graduated in 1958. Studied voice at the Eastman School of Music and performed in several school musical productions.

1941–1958 Summered with her family at Higgins Lake in Michigan.

1958 Left Rochester for Vassar College to study music and literature.

1960 Began experimenting in oil painting. Traveled by car across the United States. Continued solo recitals at Vassar College and performed at Yale University. Published the first of five editions of a contemporary poetry journal entitled i.e.

1961 Left Vassar College and moved to New York. Attended the New School for Social Research graduating in 1962 with a Bachelor of Arts in American Literature. Continued her interest in Emerson who, along with the other Transcendentalists, was the subject of her senior thesis. Studied painting briefly with Julian Levi and the history, philosophy and psychology of art with Rudolf Arnheim. Began vacationing at Lake Placid in the Adirondack Mountains.

1963 Married Peter Wendt. Visited the Florida wilderness areas and began a series of slides of the sky alone that would later influence the **Cloud Series** of paintings.

1964 First solo exhibition in March at the Carl Solway Gallery (formerly Flair House Galleries), Cincinnati, Ohio.

1961 The Lower East Side studio, New York

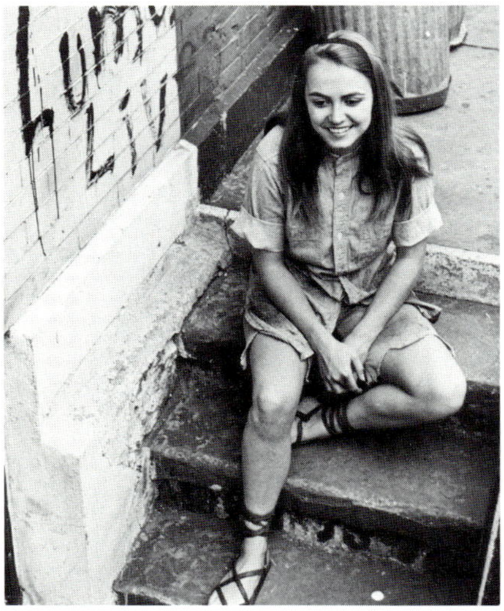

1962 In the Berkshire Mountains

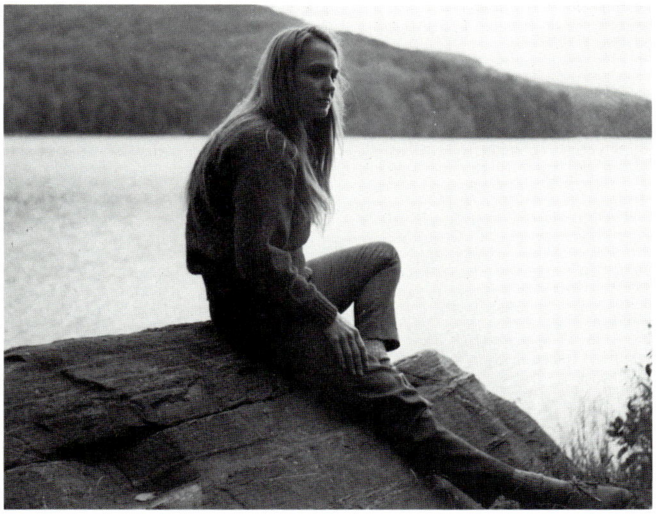

1966 First of three annual exhibitions at The York Gallery, New York. Visited Haiti, her first trip outside the United States.

1967 Included in museum exhibitions: "Paintings and Sculpture Today" at the Indianapolis Museum of Art (formerly the Herron Museum of Art), Indiana and "Dealers' Choice" at the Gallery of Modern Art, New York. Largest painting to date, **The Mendon Diptych,** acquired by the Memorial Art Gallery, Rochester, New York for its permanent collection. Toured Alaska by car and bush plane on a five-week camping expedition that initiated the **Alaska Series** of paintings and prompted an interest in drawing and photography.

1968 & 1970 Solo exhibitions at the Hunter Gallery, Aspen, Colorado.

1968 Camped for four weeks in the Southwest which provided the initial impetus for the **Mesa Series** of the following decade.

1969 First retrospective, forty-five paintings chosen from eight years of work, in April at The Saginaw Art Museum, Michigan. Celebrated the birth of her daughter, Alyssa Taylor Wendt, on November 16.

1970 & 1972 Solo exhibitions at The Schuman Gallery, Rochester, New York. Made first of several houseboating trips in the Bahamas.

1973 Moved north from New York to the Hudson River town of Garrison.

1974 Solo exhibition at the Lake Placid Center for Music, Drama and Art. Spent a week in Casablanca, Morocco and drove through the Atlas Mountains.

1975 & 1977 Solo exhibitions at the Christopher Gallery, New York.

1967 Camping in Alaska

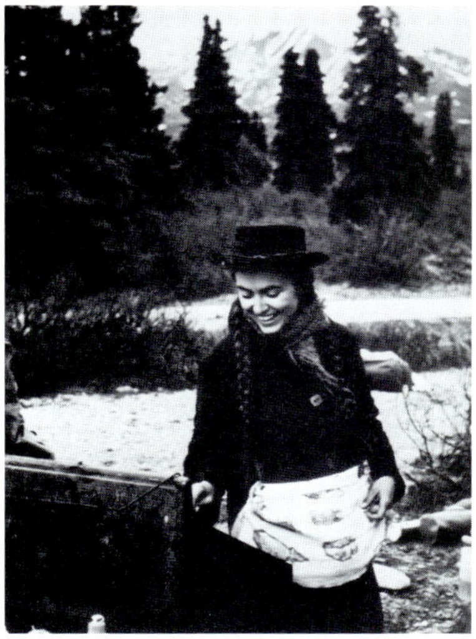

1970 The Union Square studio, New York

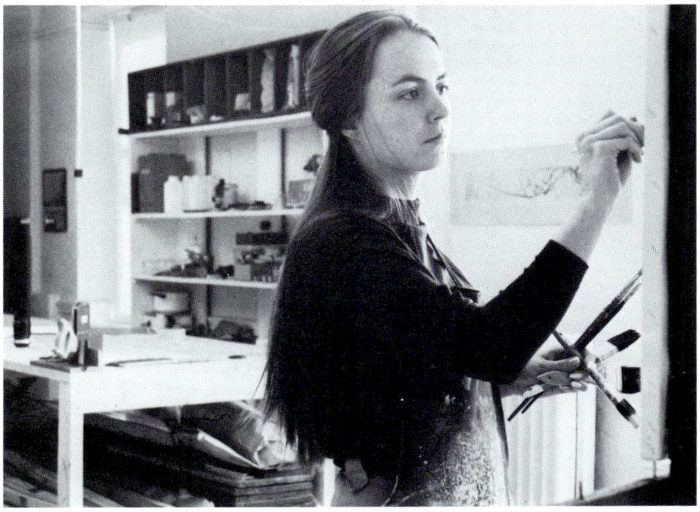

1975 Solo exhibition at the Elaine Horwitch Gallery, Scottsdale, Arizona. Traveled to London specifically to see the major retrospective of Joseph Turner's work at the Royal Academy of Arts.

1976, 1980 & 1982 Solo exhibitions at the Oxford Gallery, Rochester, New York.

1978 Solo exhibition at The Miller Gallery, Cincinnati, Ohio. Sailed up the Inland Passage to Alaska and drove for the first time through the Canadian Rockies. The trip prompted a revival of the **Alaska Series.**

1978 & 1980 Solo exhibitions at the Suzanne Brown Gallery, Scottsdale, Arizona.

1978 Compiled and privately published an extensively illustrated genealogy of her family, **All of Us: A Biographical History of John Jacob Bausch and his descendants from 1830 to 1978.**

1979 Completed **Liberation,** 108" by 144", her largest corporate commission to date, for the Third National Bank and Trust Company in Dayton, Ohio in coordination with the installation of three major sculptural works by Buckminster Fuller. To date representation in corporate collections included Bank of America, Houston; Valley National Bank, Phoenix; Honeywell, Inc., Minneapolis; Central Trust Company, Cincinnati; Bausch & Lomb Inc., Lincoln First Trust Company and Xerox, Rochester. Moved to Scottsdale, Arizona, with her daughter, Alyssa.

1979 Published first editions of lithographs at Southwest Graphics in Scottsdale.

1981 In the Arizona desert

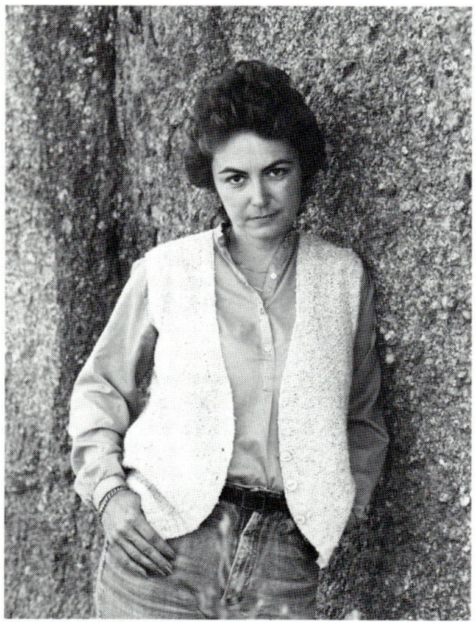

Rollie McKenna

1982 On the Colorado River

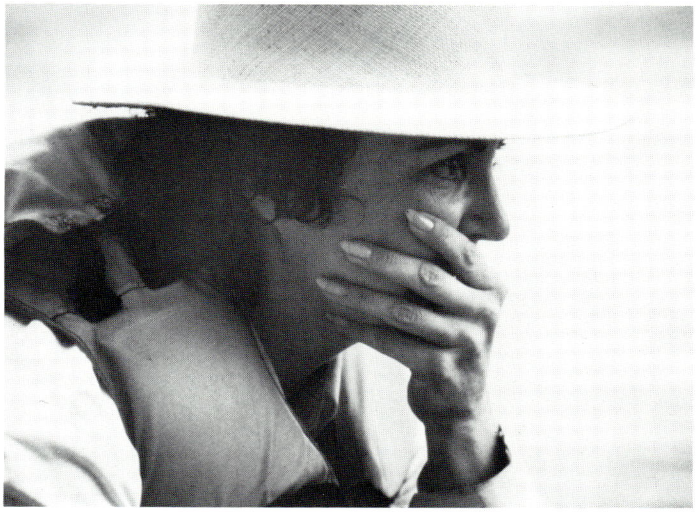

Sheila Kollasch

1980 Solo exhibition at The Munson Gallery, Santa Fe, New Mexico. Began **Acceleration Series** of paintings. Divorced Peter Wendt.

1981 Solo exhibition at the C. G. Rein Galleries, Minneapolis, Minnesota. Arranged to spend the summer in Europe and the British Isles under the sponsorship of fifteen of her collectors.

1982 Completed the **British Isles Series** of paintings. Solo exhibition at the C. G. Rein Galleries, Scottsdale, Arizona. Joined a ten-day rafting expedition on the Colorado River in the Grand Canyon along with thirty-five other artists. Began the **Windows, Rearview Mirrors and Ghosts Series.**

1965–1983 Exhibited in group shows at Adelle M. Fine Art, Dallas; A. R. T. Beasley Gallery, San Diego; Art Resources Gallery, Denver; Arwin Galleries, Detroit; Gallery One, Petoskey; Gallery Henoch, New York; Hall Gallery, Fort Worth; Janet Fleischer Gallery, Philadelphia; Julia Black Gallery, Taos; Mickelson Gallery, Washington; Nantucket Gallery, Nantucket; Naples Art Gallery, Naples; Peter M. David Gallery, Minneapolis, and Sebastian-Moore Gallery, Denver.

1983 Solo exhibition at the C. G. Rein Galleries, Houston, Texas. Traveled to the Yucatan Peninsula, Mexico to see the Mayan ruins.

1984 Retrospective exhibition of her work opened at the Rochester Museum and Science Center and traveled to other museums and art centers in the United States.

1983 The Kaibab studio, Scottsdale

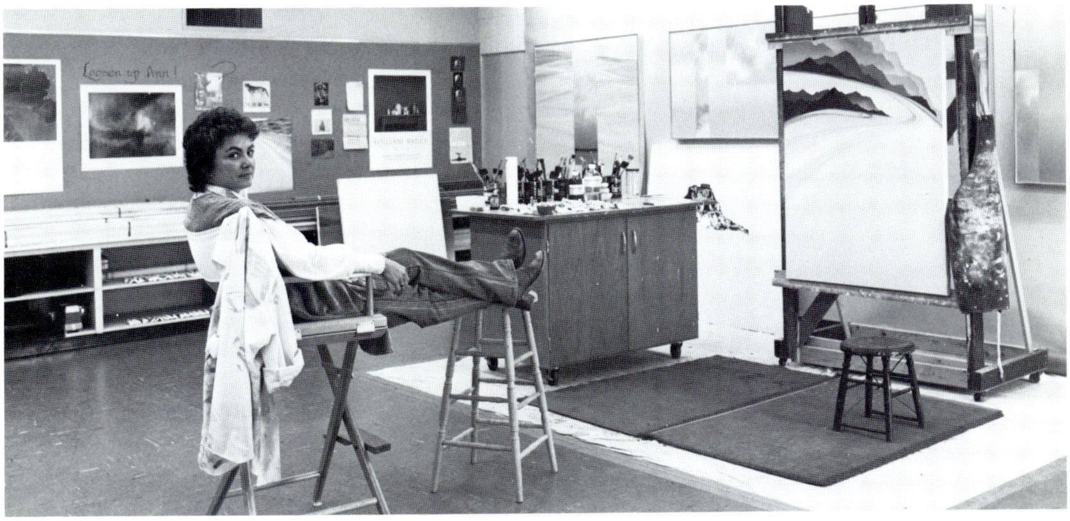

James Cowlin

The production of this book was coordinated by Brenda Locke to whom a special note of thanks is given for her enthusiasm and intelligence.

B.C.

The first edition of **THE REACH OF SOLITUDE: The Paintings of Ann Taylor** consisted of four thousand copies. It was produced in Phoenix, Arizona in 1983. The book was designed by Richard F. Smith, Graphics West Design Associates. It was printed in Novarese typeface on eighty-pound Productolith Dull Book by Imperial Litho/ Graphics, Inc. under the direction of Russell Kurtz and bound by Roswell Bookbinding.

A limited edition of one hundred and fifty copies in a special binding, each including an original handprinted lithograph, were inscribed by the artist.